The Cambridge English Course

This book contains the third third of the complete edition of *The Cambridge English Course*, Student's Book 1.

1 Student's Book

Michael Swan and Catherine Walter

Cambridge University Press

Cambridge   London   New York   New Rochelle   Melbourne   Sydney

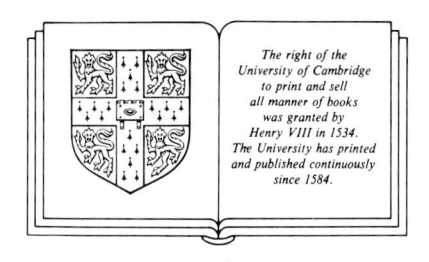

Published by the Press Syndicate of the University of Cambridge
The Pitt Building, Trumpington Street, Cambridge CB2 1RP
32 East 57th Street, New York, NY10022, USA
10 Stamford Road, Oakleigh, Melbourne 3166, Australia

© Cambridge University Press 1984, 1986

Complete edition first published 1984
This split edition first published 1986
Reprinted 1986

Designed by John Youé and Associates, Croydon, Surrey
Typeset by Text Filmsetters Limited, London
Origination by Vyner Litho Plates Limited, London
Printed in Great Britain by Blantyre Printing and Binding, Glasgow

ISBN 0 521 28908 4 Student's Book 1

Split edition:
ISBN 0 521 31028 8 Part A
ISBN 0 521 31029 6 Part B
ISBN 0 521 31030 X Part C

ISBN 0 521 28910 6 Teacher's Book 1
ISBN 0 521 28909 2 Practice Book 1
ISBN 0 521 27865 1 Test Book 1
ISBN 0 521 24703 9 Cassette Set 1
ISBN 0 521 26223 2 Student's Cassette 1

Copyright
The law allows a reader to make a single copy of part of a book for purposes of private study. It does not allow the copying of entire books or the making of multiple copies of extracts. Written permission for any such copying must always be obtained from the publisher in advance.

Authors' acknowledgements

A book like this necessarily owes a great deal to a great many people. Our thanks to:

Alan Maley, for the splendid seminar programme which he organized at the British Council, Paris, in the 1970s. This was an unparalleled source of information, ideas and inspiration.

Donn Byrne, Alan Duff, Alan Maley, Heather Murray, Penny Ur and Jane Wright, for specific ideas and exercises which we have borrowed.

The many other people – too many to acknowledge – whose ideas have influenced our work, including all the colleagues and students from whom we have learnt.

Those institutions and teachers who were kind enough to work with the Pilot Edition of this course, and whose comments have done so much to shape the final version.

Peter Roach and Ian Thompson for their expert and sensible help with the phonetic transcription.

John Youé, Steve Williams, Gillian Clack, Richard Child, Chris Rawlings, Clifford Webb and Diana Dobson of Youé and Spooner Limited, our designers, for their unfailing understanding, good humour and expertise.

John and Angela Eckersley, and the staff of the Eckersley School of English, Oxford, for making it possible for us to try out parts of the book in their classrooms.

Steve Dixon, Lorna Higgs, John Peake, Pat Robbins, Fran Searson, Ann Swan, Ruth Swan, Heather and Paul Teale, Sue Ward, Adrian Webber, and Susan Webber, for agreeing to be quizzed and questioned within earshot of our microphones.

Judy Haycox, Joanne Haycox, Susan Webber and Helen Walter, for invaluable domestic support during a trying period.

Mark, for patience and good humour beyond the call of duty.

And finally, to Adrian du Plessis, Peter Donovan, Barbara Thomas and Peter Ducker of Cambridge University Press: few authors can have been so fortunate in their publishers.

Contents

> **Note**
> Page numbering from the complete edition of Student's Book 1 has been retained throughout.

Map of Book 1 4

Unit 23 Instructions... 94
Unit 24 Getting around 98
Unit 25 Knowing about the future 102
Unit 26 Feelings.. 106
Unit 27 Movement and action............................... 110
Unit 28 Parts 114
Unit 29 Predictions 118
Unit 30 Useful; useless 122
Unit 31 Self and others.. 126
Unit 32 Revision and fluency practice 130

Summaries 153
Acknowledgements
Phonetic symbols and Irregular verbs

Map of Book 1*

In Unit	Students will learn to	Students will learn to talk about
23	Give instructions and advice.	Sports; position, direction and change of position; cooking.
24	Make requests; ask for and give information.	Hotels; public transport; air travel; place and direction.
25	Talk about plans; make predictions.	Plans; small ads; travel.
26	Talk about problems; express sympathy; make suggestions; express and respond to emotions; describe relationships.	Common physical problems; personal relationships.
27	Narrate.	Ways of travelling; speed; how things are done.
28	Describe objects; narrate.	Education systems; quantity; shapes; parts of things; position; structuring of time-sequences; daily routines.
29	Predict; warn; raise and counter objections.	Danger; horoscopes.
30	Classify; make and accept apologies; correct misunderstandings; complain.	Need; importance; use and usefulness; shopping.
31	Make, accept and decline offers; ask for and analyse information.	Reciprocal and reflexive action; self and others; social situations; possession.
REVISION 32	Express obligation and opinions; other functions dependent on your choice of activities.	Correctness; other areas depending on activities chosen.

*This 'map' of the course should be translated into the students' language where possible.

Students will learn these grammar points	Students will study these aspects of pronunciation
Imperatives; *if*-clauses; prepositions of place and movement; *should* + infinitive; grammar of written and spoken instructions.	Letter *o* pronounced /ɒ/ and /ʌ/.
Have to; infinitive of purpose; preposition + *-ing* form; prepositions of place and direction.	Devoicing of /v/ in *have to*.
Going to; connectors in paragraphs; paragraph-structuring adverbials; infinitives and *-ing* forms.	Spellings of /ɜː/; pronunciation of *going to*.
It + Simple Present + *me*; *It makes me* + adjective.	'Long' and 'short' vowels.
Superlatives; different meanings of *get*; adverbs of manner; adjectives and adverbs.	Decoding fast speech.
Quantifying expressions; fractions; *at the top/bottom* etc.; *in* and *at* for time; structuring with adverbs and conjunctions.	Identifying unstressed words; word-stress and /ə/.
Will + infinitive; *get lost/killed/married*.	Pronunciation of *w, 'll, won't*.
X uses y to do z (with); *x does y with z*; words having more than one grammatical function.	Use of stress for emphasis and contrast.
Reflexive/emphatic pronouns; *each other*; *somebody else*; *Shall I . . . ?*; *I'd love/prefer/like*; *to* as pro-verb; *whose*; *somebody/anybody* etc.	Strong and weak pronunciations of *shall*; decoding unstressed words in fast speech.
(Revision) *have to*; *should*; verb tenses; question forms; adjectives; and other structures dependent on students' choice of activities.	

Unit 23

Instructions

A How to do it

1 Here is some advice about running. Some of it is good, and some is not. Which sentences give you good advice?

RUNNING① – DOs and DON'Ts

Wear good running shoes.
Run early in the morning – it's better.
Wear comfortable clothing②.
Always warm up③ before you run.
Always run with somebody – never run alone.
Rest every ten minutes or so.
Walk for a few minutes after you finish.

Don't run if you feel tired.
Never drink water while you are running.
Don't run until two hours after eating.
Don't run if you have got a cold④.
Don't run fast downhill⑤.
Don't run if you are over 50.
Don't run on roads in fog⑥.

When you have finished the exercise, listen to some British people trying to do it.

2 Work in groups. Think of some advice (good or bad) for one of the following.

– a tourist in your country
– somebody who is learning to drive
– somebody who is learning your language
– somebody who is learning English
– somebody who wants to get rich
– somebody who wants more friends

Make a list of three (or more) DOs and three (or more) DON'Ts.

3 Listen, and try to draw the picture.

4 Work in groups.
One student draws a simple picture, but does not show it to the others.
He or she gives the others instructions, and they try to draw the same picture.

5 Say these words after the recording or your teacher.

1. fog   hot   long   doctor   dollar   office
2. comfortable   front   another   brother

**Find some more words that go in group 1.
Can you find any more that go in group 2?**

B Be careful!

1 Put the following expressions into the pictures.

> Please hurry!   Take your time.   Don't worry.   Look.   Come in.   Wait here, please.
> Be careful.   Follow me, please.   Look out!

2 Work in groups. Prepare and practise a very short sketch using one or more of the expressions from Exercise 1.

3 Listen to the recording.
Write ✓ every time you hear an imperative (like *Walk, Come in, Be careful*), and ✗ every time you hear a negative imperative (like *Don't run, Don't worry*).
Listen again, and then try to remember some of the imperatives and negative imperatives.

Unit 23C

C On and off

1 Look at the picture. Where are things? Where should they be? Example:

'There's a chair on the piano. It should be on the floor.'

| Useful words: | on | in | under | by |

2 Some friends are going to help you to put things in the right places.
What will you say to them? Example:

'Could you take the chair off the piano and put it by the window?'

| Useful words: | take | put | off | out of | in(to) |

3 Listen to the song and try to put in the missing words. Your teacher will help you with vocabulary.

'I dropped my ....'
'Pick .... up, pick .... up
and put .... away in .... closet.'

'I dropped my ....'
'Pick .... up, pick .... up
and throw .... away .... basket.'

'I dropped my ....'
'Pick .... up, pick .... up
and wash .... clean in the ....'

'I dropped my dolly.'
'Pick .... up, pick .... up
and .... back in .... cradle.'

'I dropped my toys.'
'Pick .... up, pick .... up
and put .... back in .... places.'

(*Pick it up* by Woody Guthrie; © copyright 1954 Folkways Music Publishers, Inc.)

D Recipes

Mushroom Salad

Ingredients
½ lb white mushrooms, very fresh
1 tablespoon lemon juice
Pepper, salt
A few chives or a little parsley
4 tablespoons olive oil

Utensils
Bowl   Fork
Clean cloth   Knife

Time
10 mins to prepare,
1½ hrs to stand.

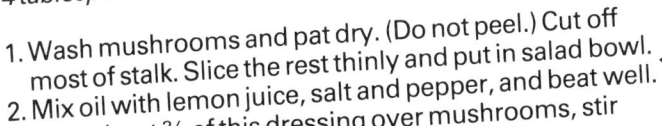

1. Wash mushrooms and pat dry. (Do not peel.) Cut off most of stalk. Slice the rest thinly and put in salad bowl.
2. Mix oil with lemon juice, salt and pepper, and beat well.
3. Pour about ⅔ of this dressing over mushrooms, stir gently and put aside for an hour.
4. Add rest of dressing and put aside again until most of dressing is absorbed, about ½ hour.
5. Meanwhile, chop chives or parsley. Sprinkle this over salad, and serve.

(from *The Beginner's Cookery Book* by Betty Falk)

1 Match each picture to one of the numbered instructions in the recipe. Use one number twice.

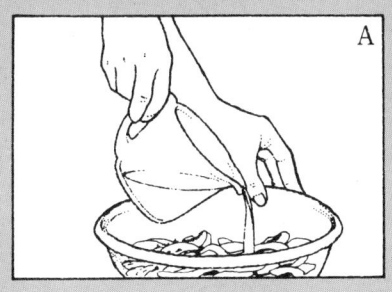

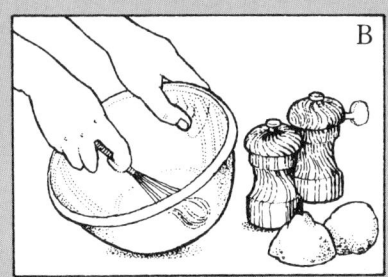

A   B   C   D   E   F

2 Listen to someone telling you how to make a mushroom salad. The grammar of the spoken recipe is different from that of the written recipe. In what ways?

3 Write a recipe (begin *Ingredients......*).
Then give instructions to another student.
(Begin '*You take...*') Here are some words you can use:
saucepan, frying-pan, casserole, oven, fry, boil, melt.

4 Look at the summary on page 153 with your teacher.

Unit 23D

Unit 24

Getting around

A A room for two nights

1 Study and practise the dialogue.

RECEPTIONIST: Can I help you?
TRAVELLER: Yes, I'd like a room, please.
RECEPTIONIST: Single or double?
TRAVELLER: Single, please.
RECEPTIONIST: For one night?
TRAVELLER: No, two nights.
RECEPTIONIST: With bath or with shower?
TRAVELLER: With bath, please. How much is the room?
RECEPTIONIST: £23 a night, including breakfast.
TRAVELLER: Can I pay by credit card?
RECEPTIONIST: Yes, of course. Could you register, please?
TRAVELLER: Pardon?
RECEPTIONIST: Could you fill in the form, please?
TRAVELLER: Oh, yes.
RECEPTIONIST: Your room number is 403. Have a good stay.
TRAVELLER: Thank you.

2 Think of other expressions that can be useful in a hotel. Ask your teacher how to say them.

3 Work with a partner. Make up a new traveller–receptionist conversation, with as many changes as possible. Your teacher will help you.

4 Answer the questions. Time-limit: five minutes.

1. What street is the Hilton Hotel in?
2. How many cars can be parked in the Hilton garage?
3. How far is the Hilton from Victoria Station?
4. How many other Hilton hotels are there in London?
5. How much do guests at the Hilton pay for children if they sleep in the same room as their parents?

Hilton International London

Hotel Features:

- Address: 22 Park Lane, London W1A 2HH, England
- Telephone: 01-493-8000 Telex: 24873 Cable: HILTELS–London
- Located in the heart of Mayfair, overlooking Hyde Park Minutes from the elegant shopping and theatre districts
- 40 minutes from Heathrow Airport, 45 minutes from London–Gatwick Airport, 5 minutes from Victoria Station
- 509 comfortable guest rooms featuring:
  individual climate control
  direct-dial telephone
  electronic locks for maximum security
  radio and taped music
  self service mini-bar
  television with in-house films
- 104 one- two- and three bedroom suites
- 5 restaurants, cocktail lounge, bar and discotheque
- 24-hour room service
- Same day laundry/valet service at no extra charge (Monday-Friday)
- Meeting facilities for up to 1000 persons
- 24-hour telex, cable, interpreter, secretarial service, typewriters, mail and postage facilities
- Pocket bleepers available for individual guest paging
- Worldwide courier service for documents guaranteeing one to three day delivery
- Teleplan – guarantees reasonable surcharges on international telephone calls
- Currency exchange at daily bank rates plus a modest handling charge of approximately 1% to cover only direct expenses
- Guest shops including beauty and barber, fashion, florist, drugstore, newsstand, speciality shops and transportation desk
- Indoor parking for 350 cars
- Hilton International Family Plan: there is no room charge for one or more children, regardless of age, when sharing the same room(s) with their parent(s) Maximum occupancy per room 3 persons

In England, there are two other fine Hilton International hotels – Hilton International Kensington on Holland Park Avenue near London's West End, and Hilton International Stratford-upon-Avon, 5 minutes from the Royal Shakespeare Theatre. And look for the new Gatwick Hilton International.

For reservations call your travel agent, any Hilton hotel or Hilton Reservation Service

B You have to change twice

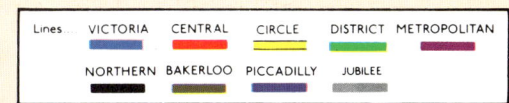

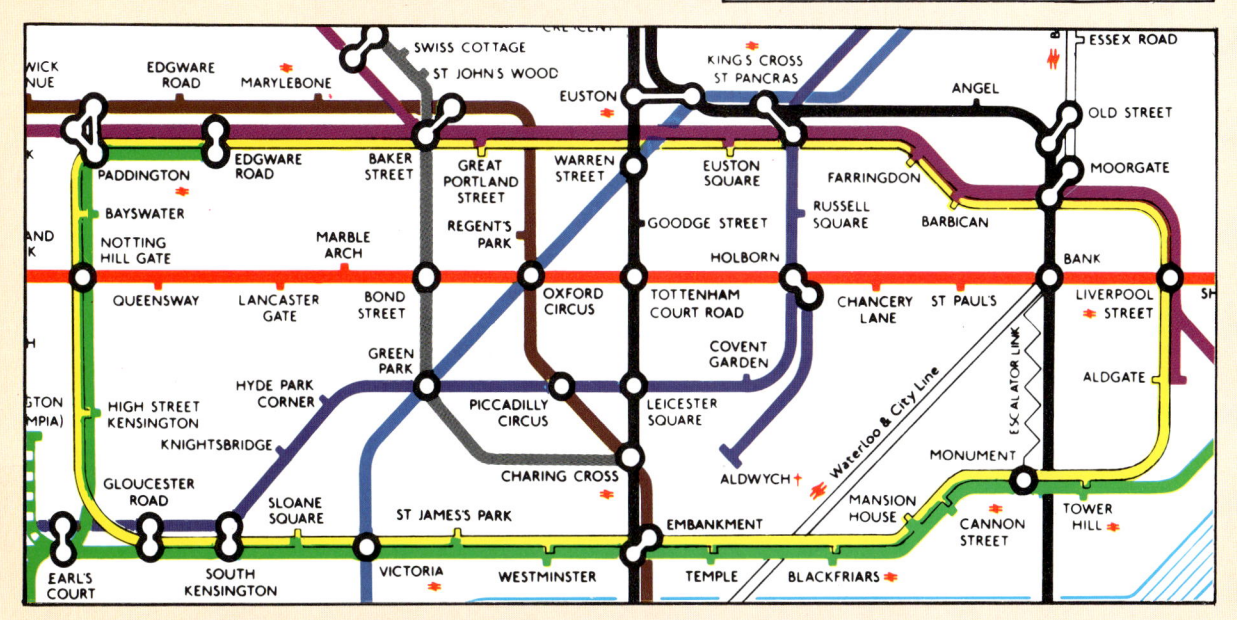

Lines: VICTORIA   CENTRAL   CIRCLE   DISTRICT   METROPOLITAN
NORTHERN   BAKERLOO   PICCADILLY   JUBILEE

1 The London Underground. True or False?

1. Baker St is on the way from Paddington to Euston Square.
2. You can get from Victoria to Baker St without changing.
3. To get from Oxford Circus to Paddington, you have to change twice.
4. Piccadilly Circus is on the way from South Kensington to Bond St.
5. You can get from Bond St to Leicester Square without changing.
6. If you go from Edgware Rd to Hyde Park Corner by the shortest way, you have to change twice.
7. You can go there by a longer way without changing.
8. Notting Hill Gate is on the same line as Holborn.
9. You can't get from Covent Garden to Victoria without changing.
10. If you travel east from Temple on the Circle Line, you can change to the Bakerloo Line at the first stop.
11. If you go from Notting Hill Gate to Green Park, you have to change at the fourth stop.
12. Knightsbridge is not on the way from Paddington to Oxford Circus.

2 Make up your own true or false sentences about the London Underground, and test other students with them.

3 San Fantastico, the capital of Fantasia, has got a new underground system, with two lines and six stops. Read the sentences and draw a map of the SF Underground.

1. Miller Rd and High St are on the same line.
2. To get from Tower Park to Royce Rd you have to change at the first stop.
3. Tower Park is on the way from Miller Rd to Ship St.
4. If you travel east from High St, Ship St is the first stop.
5. High St is on the same line as Green St.
6. You can go from Royce Rd to Green St without changing.

4 Do number 1 *or* number 2.

1. If all the students in the class are from the same place, make up true or false sentences about the transport system in your own city/country.
2. If the students in the class are from different places, tell the other students two things about the transport system in your city/country.

Unit 24C

C Flight 3 to Hong Kong

1 Which picture?

1. Your passport and boarding card, please, sir.
2. British Airways Flight 3 to Hong Kong boarding now at Gate 11.
3. British Airways announce the arrival of Flight 623 from Geneva.
4. I'd like to change my reservation, please.
5. Have you any hand baggage, madam?

2 What do these mean? Make sure you know. Then find each one in the timetable.

| British Airways flight number 3 | arrival time | Wednesday | departure time | Monday |
| Boeing 747 Jumbo Jet plane | stopping at | Sunday | minutes | minimum |

LONDON – HONG KONG 747

DEPART London, Heathrow Airport, Terminal 3 (Minimum check-in time 60 mins; BA First & Club class 45 mins)
ARRIVE Hong Kong, Kai Tak Airport

Frequency	Aircraft Dep	Arr	Via	Transfer Times	Flight	Aircraft	Class & Catering
Mo	1025	0835†	Abu Dhabi		BA3	747	PCM ✕
Tu	1700	1535†	Bombay		BA3	747	PCM ✕
We	1025	1035†	Rome, Bahrain		BA3	747	PCM ✕
Th	1700	1535†	Bombay		BA3	747	PCM ✕
Fr	1025	0835†	Abu Dhabi		BA3	747	PCM ✕
Sa	1700	1645†	Rome, Calcutta		BA3	747	PCM ✕
Su	1700	1520†	Bahrain		BA3	747	PCM ✕

† – Next day

3 Answer the questions by looking at the timetable, and make new questions to ask other students.

1. What time does the Hong Kong flight leave London on Tuesdays?
2. What is the flight number?
3. How often does the flight go via Abu Dhabi?
4. What time do flights via Bombay arrive in Hong Kong?
5. On what days can you go from London to Hong Kong via Rome?
6. Where does the flight stop on Wednesdays?
7. By what time must you check in for the Wednesday flight?

4 Listen to the announcements and complete the sentences.

1. Passengers for Birmingham on Flight BD .... – this flight is now boarding at gate number ....
2. British Midland passengers to East Midlands on .... BD .... – this flight is now boarding at ....
3. Would Mr Mattox travelling to .... please contact the British Airways .... office opposite island J on the .... floor?
4. Would Mr Rowley from .... please .... British Midland .... ?

5 Listen to the recording. How many words are there in each sentence? What are they? (Contractions like *don't*, *I've* count as two words.)

D Walk along the river bank…

1 Treasure hunt. The treasure is buried under one of the trees, at A, B, C, D, E, F, G or H. Follow the clues and find it. Start by reading clue number 6.

1. Go to the nearest railway station. Go into the station.
2. Keep straight on until you see the next clue.
3. Climb up on to the railway line.
4. Turn left and walk along the railway line until you see the next clue.
5. Turn right. Go to the nearest crossroads and turn right. The treasure is under the second tree on the right.
6. Go straight on over the bridge to the crossroads.
7. Walk back and read the last clue again.
8. Go into the nearest field. The next clue is under the first tree on the right.
9. This clue says the same as number 13.
10. Walk along the river bank to the next bridge.
11. Get on the next train; get off at the other station.
12. There's a train coming. Turn to your left and get off the railway line.
13. Go under the bridge. The next clue is just on the other side.
14. Turn left and go to the second tree on the right.
15. Go straight out of the field and take the shortest way to the river by road. The next clue is at the crossroads.
16. You're lost.

2 Describe the route you took to the treasure.

I went straight over the bridge to the crossroads; then I turned left and went to the second tree on the right;

3 Look at the summary on page 153 with your teacher.

Unit 25
Knowing about the future

A This is going to be my room

1 What are your plans for this evening? Are you going to do any of these things?

write letters   see a film
play cards   see friends
watch TV   wash your hair
listen to music   study

Examples:
'I'm going to write letters.'
'I'm not going to watch TV.'

2 This is going to be your house. It isn't finished yet. Look at the plan and decide what the various rooms are going to be and how you are going to furnish them. Include some or all of the following: kitchen, bathroom(s), toilet(s), bedrooms, living room, dining room, study, playroom, and any other rooms that you want. If you haven't got enough rooms, put on another floor.

When you have finished, work with another student and tell him/her what the rooms are going to be. Example:

'This is going to be the kitchen.'

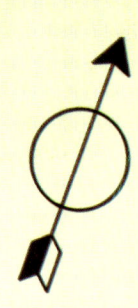

3 Listen to some people talking about their plans. What do you think these words mean?

exercise   kid   shout   couple   less

4 Have you got any plans for the next year or so? Are you going to make any changes in your life? What? Think of something that you are never going to do again in your life.

5 Pronunciation. Say these words.

certain   first   bird   dirty   stir   third
thirty   thirsty   shirt   turn   hurt   Thursday
work   word   world   worst
learn   heard   early   year

B It's going to rain

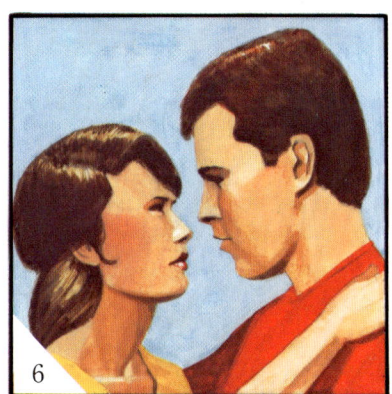

Unit 25B

1 Look at the pictures. What is going to happen? (If you don't know the words, use your dictionary or ask your teacher.)

2 Read the advertisement. Then make up advertisements yourselves (working in groups) to get people to join your holiday trip.

HOLIDAY IN SCOTLAND
We are organizing a holiday walking tour in the North of Scotland.
We are going to cover 150 miles of mountainous country in ten days.
It's going to be hard work.
It's going to be tough.
You're going to be wet, cold and tired a lot of the time.
But it's going to be fun!
If you are young and fit, and if you like beautiful places – why not join us? Cost £38 inclusive.
For more details, write Box 1346, *Edinburgh Times*.

We are organizing a trip to
....
We are going to ....
....
It's going to be ....
....
It's going to be ....
....
And/But it's going to be ...
....
If you are ....
.....................................,
....................................., and
.....................................,
why not join us?
Cost: £............ inclusive.

3 Mime a person who is going to do something. The other students will try to say what you are going to do.

You're going to swim.

103

Unit 25C

C Why? To...

1 You go to a university to study. Why do you go to these places?

2 Can you make five more sentences like these?

'People don't go to Nigeria to ski.'
'People don't go to Iceland to drink wine.'

3 Why are you learning English?

4 Mr Andrews is an English tourist who is travelling to Eastern Europe tomorrow. Just now he's having breakfast at home. After breakfast, he's going out to do a lot of things. (For example, he's going to Harrods to buy a suitcase.) Look at the pictures, and then write a paragraph to say where he's going and why. Connect your sentences with *First of all, then, and then, after that, next, tomorrow*.

Where?

Why?

D To and -ing

INFINITIVE WITHOUT *TO* (**Examples:** go, speak)

Used after 'auxiliary verbs':

can	*I can speak German.*
could	*Could you speak more slowly?*
will	*It will rain tomorrow.*
should	*You should be at home.*
do	*Does he smoke?*
	Don't stop.
let's	*Let's have a drink.*

INFINITIVE WITH *TO* (**Examples:** to go, to speak)

Used in many kinds of sentence. After:

something	*Would you like something to eat?*
nothing	*There's nothing to do.*
anything	*Have you got anything to drink?*
I'm sorry	*I'm sorry to trouble you.*

Also used after many verbs:

would like	*Would you like to dance?*
would love	*I'd love to speak German.*
hope	*I hope to see you soon.*
want	*I don't want to go home.*
have	*You have to change at the next station.*

And used to say why we do things:

'Why did you come here?' 'To see you.'

-*ING* FORM (**Examples:** going, speaking)

Used in many kinds of sentence. After some verbs:

like	*I like speaking French.*
love	*I love going to the theatre.*
hate	*I hate waiting for people.*

And after all prepositions:

after	*After seeing the doctor I felt better.*
before	*Before going to bed I usually read the paper.*
for	*Thank you for inviting me.*
at	*She's good at swimming.*
without	*Can you get there without changing?*

And in the Present Progressive tense:

'What are you doing?' 'I'm writing letters.'

---

1 Put in the infinitive with or without *to*.

1. Can you ....? (swim)
2. Have you got anything ....? (read)
3. Could I .... to Lucy? (speak)
4. I don't .... (understand)
5. I'd like .... you again. (see)
6. I hope .... to America in May. (go)
7. It takes a long time .... English. (learn)
8. Let's .... (dance)
9. Why don't we .... a drink? (have)

2 Put in the infinitive or the *-ing* form.

1. Would you like ....? (dance)
2. Do you like ....? (dance)
3. Can you .... chess? (play)
4. Thank you for .... me. (help)
5. I'm very bad at .... (ski)
6. You can't live without .... (eat)
7. How do you .... 'please'? (pronounce)
8. Could you .... me the time? (tell)
9. I love .... (cook)
10. My husband can't .... (cook)

3 Listen to the song. When the recording stops, say what is coming next.

4 Look at the summary on page 154 with your teacher.

Unit 26

Feelings

A I feel ill

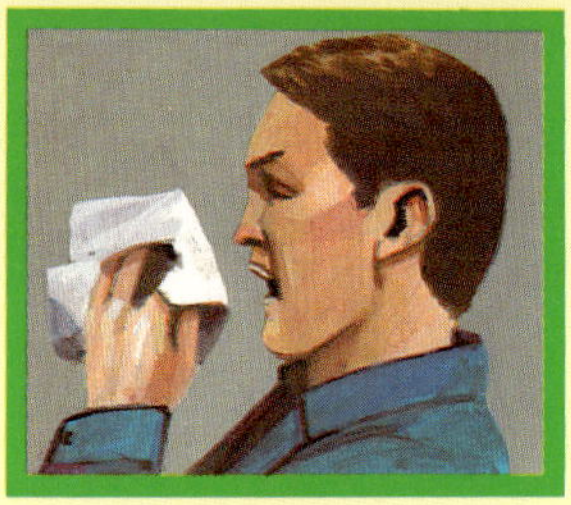

1. I've got a cold. 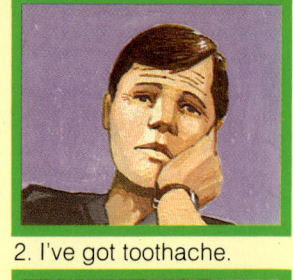
2. I've got toothache. 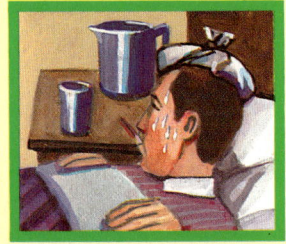
3. I've got a temperature. 
4. I've got flu. 
5. I've got a headache. 
6. My leg hurts.

a. Why don't you go home and lie down?
b. Why don't you take an aspirin? 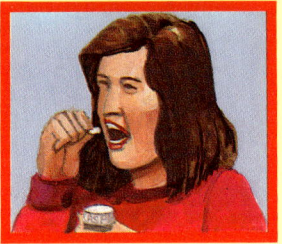
c. Why don't you see the doctor? 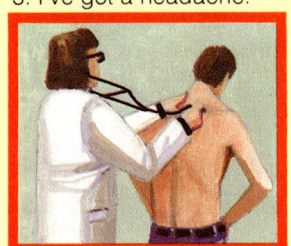
d. Why don't you see the dentist? 

1 Match the letters and the numbers. You can use a dictionary.

2 Ask and answer.

'How do you feel?'
'I'm very hungry, and my arm hurts a bit.'

3 Listen to the dialogue. Then change some of the words and practise it with a partner. Your teacher will help you.

WOMAN: Good morning, Mr Culham. How are you?
MAN: I feel ill.
WOMAN: I *am* sorry. What's the matter?
MAN: My eyes hurt, and I've got a bad headache.
WOMAN: Well, why don't you take an aspirin?
MAN: That's a good idea.

4 At the doctor's. Write the other half of this dialogue. Work in groups if you can. Your teacher will help you.

DOCTOR: Good morning. What's the problem?
YOU: Well, ...
DOCTOR: I see. Does it / Do they hurt very badly?
YOU: ....
DOCTOR: How long have you had this?
YOU: ....
DOCTOR: Yes, right. I'd like to examine you, then. Mmm... Mmm...
YOU: ....?
DOCTOR: No, it doesn't look too bad. Here's a prescription for some medicine. Phone me if you're not better by the day after tomorrow.
YOU: ....
DOCTOR: Goodbye.
YOU: ....

5 Ask your teacher how to say three other words you can use at the doctor's.

B It frightens me

Unit 26B

1 Choose one of the pictures above. Ask other students: *'How do you feel about this picture?'* Examples of answers:

'It frightens me.'   'It depresses me.'   'It makes me angry.'   'I think it's lovely.'   'I think it's interesting.'   'I think it's disgusting.'   'I don't like it much.'

2 Think of four other things and write about your feelings towards them. You can use words from Exercise 1 or from the box. Examples:

Unemployment worries me.
I think cigarettes are disgusting.

worries	happy	funny	wonderful
bores	unhappy	pretty	beautiful
		stupid	exciting
		nice	

3 Survey. Ask other students about one of the things you wrote about. Report the results to the class.

4 Put a word or words in each blank. Then listen and practise.

TOM: ...., Jill. How ....?
JILL: .... depressed.
TOM: I .... What's the matter?
JILL: .... boyfriend isn't here. .... America.
TOM: Oh dear! Well, ... you .... to .... dinner with us tonight?
JILL: That's .... nice of you, Tom. ...., I ....
TOM: See you .... seven o'clock, then. ....
JILL: ....

5 Work with a partner. Make and practise a new conversation using words from the lesson.

107

Unit 26C

Do you like your boss?

WE ASKED THREE PEOPLE:

Celia

I really like my boss. She's a lovely person, very easy to work for, very fair. She always asks what I think before she changes anything. If there's a problem, we solve it together. She never gets angry. I trust her, and she trusts me. It's a pleasure to work for her.

George

I get on all right with my .... He .... worry about .... details of .... work; he's .... fair, and .... gives me a lot .... freedom. .... like that. It .... me a bit angry when he .... me more work .... I can .... I don't .... he understands that parts .... my job .... very difficult. But on the whole, I don't .... we .... on too badly.

Lesley

I .... job, ... can't stand .... difficult .... talk .... really listen. And he's not .... : *he* can make mistakes, and that's all right; but .... , he .... angry. It .... when .... *me* angry when he changes his mind about really .... again and again. I can't leave .... right now, ... really fed up.

1 Read Celia's text; put one word in each blank in George's text; put one or more words in each blank in Lesley's text. You can use a dictionary.

2 Think of one person you know (boss/sister/uncle etc.). Write four sentences about how you get on with that person. Try to use words from the texts.

3 Work in groups. Each person reads the sentences from Exercise 2 and the others ask questions. Some words you can use in your questions:

| easy/difficult to talk to | angry | problems |
| trust | freedom | listen | mistakes |

4 Copy this list. Then listen, and mark off each expression when you hear it.

in a pub   he's smashing   sense of humour
easy to get on with   very fair   when I first came
everything that I needed to know
wasn't unfair   I made mistakes   very good to me

How does the person feel about her boss — more like Celia, more like George or more like Lesley?

108

D Love at first sight

1 Which people do you think go with text 1? Which people do you think go with text 2? Write a text for the third couple.

A B C

D E F

1. We've been married for 15 years. We met on holiday in the mountains, and it was love at first sight. We've had a few problems over the years, but we're still happy to be together. We do nearly everything together.

2. We both had terrible first marriages. It made us appreciate each other much more. We've been together for four years now. We don't spend all our time together, but we're happy to share a lot of things.

2 How does -e change the pronunciation?

WITHOUT -e:	fat	cat	am	plan	hat	NOW PRONOUNCE:	man same take that
WITH -e:	gate	late	name	plane	hate		make bad lemonade bale safe tap tape
WITHOUT -e:	sit	in	begin	if	swim	NOW PRONOUNCE:	fit inside still mile hid
WITH -e:	invite	fine	wine	wife	time		ride tide like pipe strip
WITHOUT -e:	stop	top	not	hot	clock	NOW PRONOUNCE:	job stone rose God
WITH -e:	hope	home	note	nose	smoke		joke dome bone on spot coke
WITHOUT -e:	bus	run	pub	sun	just	NOW PRONOUNCE:	much fuse cube cub
WITH -e:	excuse	June	tube	rude	use		fuss tune gun fun duke luck
EXCEPTIONS:	some	come	one	have	give	live	love

3 Look at the summary on page 155 with your teacher.

Unit 27

Movement and action

A How to get from A to B

1 Travelling. You can often say the same thing in two different ways. Try to complete the table.

ride	= go on horseback
....	= go on foot
drive	= go ....
fly	= ....
cycle	= ....

Other expressions:
hitchhike   go by boat   go by bus
go by train   go by motorbike

2 A man makes a journey across Britain. He uses several different forms of transport. Listen, and say how he is travelling.

3 This is the story of the man's journey. Fill in the missing words.

boat	broke down	drove	fast	flew
hitchhiking	motorbike	one day	packed
rode	so	so	so	train	walked
when	who	worse

Paul Lewis lives in the south of England; he has a brother John, ... lives on Barra, a small island near the west coast of Scotland. .... a friend of John's telephoned to say John was very ill, and he wanted Paul with him. Paul .... as .... as he could, caught the next .... to Heathrow Airport, and .... to Glasgow. There he hired a car and .... off to catch the .... for Barra. Unfortunately the car .... three miles from the ferry. Paul tried ...., but he couldn't get a lift, ... he .... to the ferry. .... he landed on Barra the island's one taxi was not there, ... he borrowed a horse and .... to John's house. John was much ...., ... Paul took his brother's .... and went to call the doctor.

4 Talk about a journey that you have made.
Example: 'When I was 16 I cycled from Munich to Cologne.'

110

B Like lightning

1 Match the words and the pictures.

a cheetah	a glacier
lightning	a racehorse
a racing pigeon	a rhinoceros
a salmon	a sprinter
a wasp	a snail

2 Lightning is the fastest of the things in the pictures. Which do you think is the next fastest? Which do you think is the slowest? Put them in order of speed.

3 Match the nouns and verbs, and guess the speeds. Example:

Lightning travels at 140,000 kilometres a second.

A cheetah   A glacier
Lightning   A racehorse
A rhinoceros
A racing pigeon
A salmon   A sprinter
A wasp   A snail

flies   gallops   runs
moves   crawls
swims   travels

at

50 metres per hour.   176kph.
36kph.   19kph.   56kph.
3mm per hour.   100kph.
36kph.   68kph.   140,000kps.

4 How fast do you think you walk, run, cycle, drive, read, breathe, . . . ?

5 Listening for information. Copy the table. Listen to today's results from the Fantasian National Games, and note the times and speeds.

EVENT	TIME	SPEED
Men's 100m		
Women's marathon		
Women's 100m swimming (freestyle)		
Downhill Alpine skiing		

6 Listening to fast speech. What is the second word in each sentence? (Contractions like *what's* count as two words.)

Unit 27B

Unit 27C

C If you press button A,...

1 *Get* has several different meanings. Put these sentences in groups, according to the meaning of *get*.

What time do you usually get up?
It's getting late.
My English is getting better.
Where can I get some cigarettes?
John got into his car and drove away.
It takes me an hour to get to work.
I get a letter from my mother every week.
The housing problem is getting worse.
If you go to the shops, can you get me some bread, please?
You've got beautiful eyes.

2 How does the machine work?

If you — press / push / pull / turn — button / lever / handle — A B C D E F — you get — a cup of coffee. / a packet of cigarettes. / a flower. / music. / a surprise. / an electric shock.

3 Where did you get...? Ask and answer.
Examples:

'Where did you get your shoes?' 'In Tokyo.'
'Where did you get your dictionary?' 'At the University Bookshop.'
'Where did you get that watch?' 'From my father.'

4 Put in *on, off, into, out of, up*.

1. What time did you get .... this morning?
2. She got .... her car and drove away.
3. I got .... my car and walked up to the front door.
4. 'Why are you late?' 'I got .... the wrong bus.'
5. We have to get .... at the next stop.

5 Put in suitable adjectives.

1. If you don't eat, you get ....
2. If you eat too much, you get ....
3. If you don't drink, you get ....
4. If you drink too much alcohol, you get ....
5. If you run a long way, you get ....
6. If you go out in the rain without an umbrella, you get ....
7. If you go out in the snow without a coat, you get ....
8. In the evening, when the sun goes down, it gets ....
9. We are all getting ....

D Please speak more slowly

1 How are the people speaking? Listen to the recording, and choose one adverb for each sentence.

coldly	kindly
sleepily	angrily
happily	

2 Now listen to the next five sentences, and find more adverbs to say how the people are speaking.

3 Now practise speaking in all ten ways. Then work with a partner and make up a short conversation. Speak coldly, or angrily, or fast,...; the other students must say how you are speaking.

4 Choose a verb and an adverb, and demonstrate or mime the action (for example: *walk happily; drink slowly*). The other students must say what you are doing, and how you are doing it.

> write   eat   drink   walk
> sing   speak   run   drive
> fly   sleep   cook   dance
> swim   smoke   type   wash
> play (the guitar/piano/etc.)

> fast   slowly   loudly   quietly
> happily   unhappily   angrily
> sleepily   coldly   kindly
> shyly   noisily   badly

You're walking happily.

5 Adjective or adverb?

1. I'm very .... with you. (angry/angrily)
2. She spoke to me .... (angry/angrily)
3. I don't think your mother drives very .... (good/well)
4. You've got a .... face. (nice/nicely)
5. I play the guitar very .... (bad/badly)
6. It's .... cold. (terrible/terribly)
7. Your father's got a very .... voice. (loud/loudly)
8. Why are you looking at me ....? (cold/coldly)
9. You speak very .... English. (good/well)
10. You speak English very .... (good/well)

6 Put the adverb in the right place.

1. He read the letter without speaking. (slowly)
   He read the letter slowly without speaking.
2. She speaks French. (badly)
3. I like dancing. (very much)
4. Please write your name. (clearly)
5. You should eat your food. (slowly)
6. She read his letter. (carefully)
7. I said 'Hello' and walked away. (coldly)

7 Spelling. Look carefully at these adverbs.

| badly | quietly | nicely | completely |
| angrily | happily | carefully | comfortably |

Now make adverbs from these adjectives.

| warm | great | extreme | sincere |
| hungry | lazy | real | terrible |

8 Look at the summary on page 155 with your teacher.

Unit 28 Parts

A Education

British education

GCE: General Certificate of Education.
There are two parts:
O Level (Ordinary Level), taken at age 16.
A Level (Advanced Level), taken at age 18.

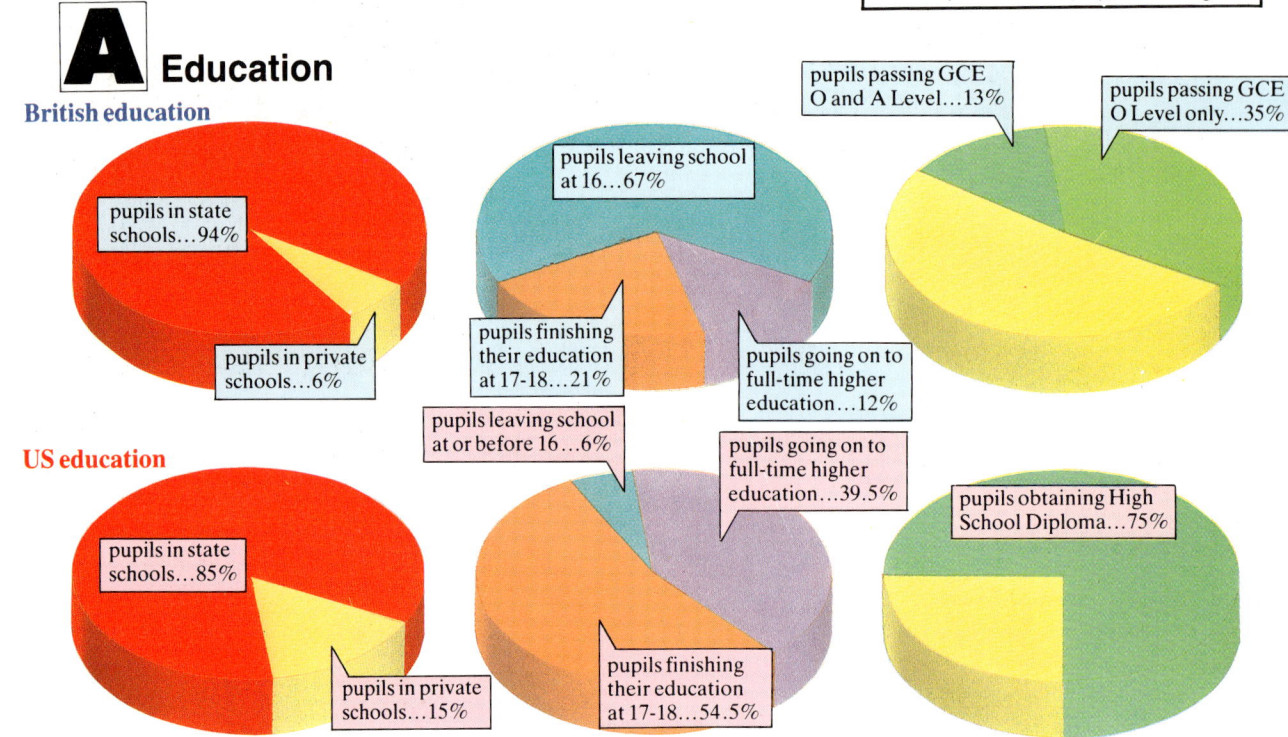

- pupils in state schools…94%
- pupils in private schools…6%
- pupils leaving school at 16…67%
- pupils finishing their education at 17-18…21%
- pupils leaving school at or before 16…6%
- pupils going on to full-time higher education…12%
- pupils passing GCE O and A Level…13%
- pupils passing GCE O Level only…35%

US education

- pupils in state schools…85%
- pupils in private schools…15%
- pupils finishing their education at 17-18…54.5%
- pupils going on to full-time higher education…39.5%
- pupils obtaining High School Diploma…75%

1 Look at the statistics. Then complete the following sentences with some of these words and expressions.

| very few   not many   some   two thirds |
| three quarters   nearly all   more |
| far more   nearly   less than |

1. ………… British pupils go to private schools.
2. ………… British pupils go to state schools.
3. ………… American than British pupils go to private schools.
4. About ………… of British pupils leave school at 16.
5. ………… American pupils leave school at 16.
6. ………… 40% of American pupils go on to full-time higher education.
7. ………… 15% of British pupils go on to full-time higher education.
8. ………… of American pupils obtain the High School Diploma.
9. ………… British pupils pass GCE A Level.
10. ………… American than British pupils go on to full-time higher education.

2 Listen to the six recorded sentences and say whether they are true or false.

3 Say something about the educational system in your country. Is it different from the British and American systems?

4 Now listen to some sentences about you and the other students.
If you think they are true, write 'true'; if not, write 'false'.
If you are not sure, write 'probably' or 'probably not'.
If you have no idea, write 'don't know'.
Examples:
1. 'You all speak some English.' *True*
2. 'Most of you smoke.' *False*
3. 'Nearly all of you are over 18.' *Don't know*

5 Ask questions to find out the truth about the statements in Exercise 4.
Tell the other students what you have found out, or make a statistical diagram and show it to the other students.

Unit 28B

B At the top on the left

1 What can you see in the pictures? Write sentences.

Picture 1 is
Picture 2 is
Picture 3 is
Picture 4 is
Picture 5 is
Picture 6 is

the top of ....
the side of ....
the front of ....
the back of ....
the bottom of ....
the corner of ....

2 Use *at the top/bottom/front/back/side(s)* in your answers to these questions.

1. Where is 6 on a clock face? Where is 12?
2. Where are the doors of a car? Of a house?
3. Where is north on a map? Where is south?
4. Where is the engine of a train?
5. Where does a bus driver sit?
6. Where is the garage of a house, usually?
7. Where are your ears?
8. Where is the index in a book?
9. Where are the stars on an American flag?

3 Read the description of the first picture; complete the description of the second picture; and write the third description yourself.

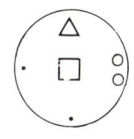

There's a big circle. Inside the circle at the top there's a small triangle. On the right at the side there are two small circles. On the left at the side there's a dot, and there's another dot at the bottom. In the middle there's a small square.

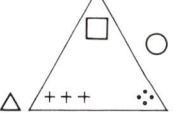

There's a big ....
.... the triangle at the
.... there's a ....
.... On the .... at the
.... there are three
............; .... the
.... the ....
there are four .... Outside the triangle on the ....
....
circle, and there's a small
.... near the bottom
left-hand ....

4 Listen to the recording and draw the picture.

5 Draw a picture. Describe it to another student and see if he/she can draw it.

Unit 28C

C The beginning of the end

1 At the beginning; in the middle; at the end.

A is at the beginning of the alphabet; M is in the middle of the alphabet; W is near the end of the alphabet. Where is C? Where is K? Where is Z?

Where is Unit 1 in this course? Unit 16? Unit 27? Unit 32?
When is June? June 15th? Three a.m.? Three p.m.? Monday?
When do people usually have soup?
When do you buy a train ticket?
When do you clap in a theatre?
When do the lights go out in a cinema?
When is a person's funeral?

2 Listen to the sounds and answer the questions.

1. When was the music loud? When was it quiet? When did somebody say 'Hello'?
2. Describe what you heard.
3. When did the telephone ring? When did somebody say 'Hello'? What else did you hear? When?
4. When did you hear the baby? When did somebody say 'Hello'? When did somebody say 'Goodbye'?
5. When did you hear the wind? the motorbike? the water? the door? What did you hear in the middle? Did the train come before or after the clock?
6. Describe what you heard. About how long did it last?

3 Pronunciation. How many words? Listen to each sentence, and write the number of words you hear.

4 Where does the stress come in these words? Where does the sound /ə/ come?

machine   about   usually
mother   photograph   alphabet
pronunciation   China   Japan
remember   cinema   America

'In the beginning was the Word.' The Bible

'In my beginning is my end.' T.S. Eliot

'This is the beginning of the end.' Talleyrand, 1812

'This is not the end. It is not even the beginning of the end. But it is, perhaps, the end of the beginning.' Churchill, 1942

'Where shall I begin, please, Your Majesty?' he asked. 'Begin at the beginning,' the King said, gravely, 'and go on till you come to the end. Then stop.' Carroll, *Alice in Wonderland*

'I like a film to have a beginning, a middle and an end, but not necessarily in that order.' Jean-Luc Godard

D What happened next?

1 Here is a story called *The Medical Book*.
Put the pictures in the right order.
Which picture comes first?
Which one is next?
Which one comes after that?...
Which one is last?

2 Read the text, and put in the following words and expressions.

| next | first | after that | then | finally |

GETTING UP
.... I get out of bed, go to the toilet, and wash and shave. .... I get dressed and brush my hair. .... I go downstairs and pick up the post and the newspaper. .... I have a long slow breakfast while I read my letters and the paper. .... I brush my teeth, put on my coat and leave for work.

3 Watch the actions, and then write down what happened. Try to use some of these words and expressions.

| first | then | next | after that | finally |

4 Put the parts of the story in order.

1. 'Didn't I tell you
2. 'Take it to the zoo,'
3. said the man,
4. a man was walking in the park
5. 'I did,'
6. He still had the penguin.
7. 'and he liked it very much.'
8. answered the policeman.
9. and asked what to do.
10. he asked.
11. 'Now I'm taking him to the cinema.'
12. the policeman saw the man again.
13. when he met a penguin.
14. Next day
15. to take that penguin to the zoo?'
16. So he took it to a policeman
17. One day

5 Look at the summary on page 156 with your teacher.

117

Unit 29

Predictions

A Are you sure you'll be all right?

1 Study and practise the dialogue.

A: I'm going to hitchhike round the world.
B: Oh, that's very dangerous.
A: No, it isn't. I'll be all right.
B: Where will you sleep?
A: Oh, I don't know. In youth hostels. Cheap hotels.
B: You'll get lost.
A: No, I won't.
B: You won't get lifts.
A: Yes, I will.
B: What will you do for money?
A: I'll take money with me.
B: You haven't got enough.
A: I'll find jobs.
B: Well,... are you sure you'll be all right?
A: Of course I'll be all right.

2 Complete these dialogues.

A: I'm .... be a racing driver.
B: Oh, that's ....
A: No, it ....
B: You'll crash. .... get killed.
A: No, ...
B: You .... find a job.
A: Yes, ... I'm a good driver.
B: Are you sure ....?
A: Of course ....

◇

A: .... a doctor.
B: .... have to study for seven years.
A: Yes, I know. I don't mind.
B: .... finish.
A: Yes, I ....
B: .... have a really hard life.
A: Yes, but it'............ interesting.
B: .... have to work very long hours.
A: I know. But I'............ enjoy it.
B: OK. If that's what you want.
A: It is.

3 Write and pronounce the contractions.

I will *I'll*
you will
he will
she will
it will
we will
they will
I will not *I won't*
you will not
it will not

4 Work with another student. Make up a short conversation beginning:

A: 'I'm going to get married.'
or A: 'I'm going to work in a circus.'
or A: 'I'm going to be a teacher.'
or A: 'I'm going to ski down Everest.'
or A: 'I'm going to be a pilot.'

5 Listen. Which sentence do you hear?

1. I stop work at six.
   I'll stop work at six.
2. You know the answer.
   You'll know the answer.
3. I have coffee for breakfast.
   I'll have coffee for breakfast.
4. You have to change at Coventry.
   You'll have to change at Coventry.
5. I drive carefully.
   I'll drive carefully.
6. I know you like my brother.
   I know you'll like my brother.

6 Where will you be this time tomorrow? What will you be doing? Example:

'I'll be at home. I'll be watching TV.'

B What will happen next?

1 Find out what these words mean. Ask your teacher or use a dictionary.

dead	prison	revolution
employer	royal	
procession	Duke	palace
mistress	famous	
successful	heart	
refuse (*verb*)	cousin	

2 Read the 'opera synopsis'. Then close your book and see how much you can remember.

3 You are at a performance of the opera *Death in Paris*. It is the interval between the second and third acts. What do you think will happen in the third act?

4 Listening. Listen to the recording. When each sentence stops, say what you think the next word will be. Example:
1. 'What's the time?' 'Three...'
   '*I think the next word will be 'o'clock'.*'

DEATH IN PARIS

**An Opera in Three Acts
by
Zoltan Grmljavina**

SYNOPSIS

ACT ONE

Anna, a beautiful 18-year-old girl, works in a shop in the old town of Goroda, in Central Moldenia. Her parents are dead; her lover, Boris, is in prison for revolutionary activities; her employer is very unkind to her. She dreams of a happier life. One day a royal procession passes in the street. The Grand Duke sees Anna and falls in love with her. He sends for her; when she goes to the palace he tells her that she must become his mistress. If not, Boris will die. Anna agrees. Boris is released from prison; in a letter Anna tells him that she can never see him again. Boris leaves Moldenia.

ACT TWO

Three years have passed. Anna and the Duke are in Paris. The Duke is dying – he has only six months to live – but the doctors have not told him. Only Anna knows the truth. One day, Anna is walking in the Tuileries when a man stops her. It is Boris. He tells her that he is now a famous artist, rich and successful. He is married to a Frenchwoman, Yvette; but in his heart he still loves Anna. 'Come away with me', he says. Anna refuses, and Boris says that he will do something terrible. At this moment, Yvette joins them. Boris tells Yvette that Anna is his cousin from Moldenia, but Yvette does not believe him.

ACT THREE

Anna and

C What do the stars say?

AQUARIUS (Jan 21–Feb 18) An old friend will come back into your life, bringing new problems. Don't make any quick decisions.

PISCES (Feb 19–Mar 20) In three days you will receive an exciting offer. But your family will make difficulties.

ARIES (Mar 21–Apr 20) Money will come to you at the end of the week. Be careful – it could go away again very fast!

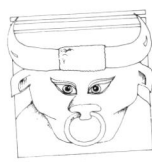

TAURUS (Apr 21–May 21) You will have trouble with a child. Try to be patient. You will have a small accident on Sunday – nothing serious.

GEMINI (May 22–June 21) This will be a good time for love, but there will be a serious misunderstanding with somebody close to you. Try to tell the truth.

CANCER (June 22–July 22) You will meet somebody who could change your life. Don't be too cautious – the opportunity won't come again.

LEO (July 23–Aug 23) Something very strange will happen next Thursday. Try to laugh about it.

VIRGO (Aug 24–Sept 23) This will be a terrible week. The weekend will be the worst time. Stay in bed on Sunday. Don't open the door. Don't answer the phone.

LIBRA (Sept 24–Oct 23) There will be bad news the day after tomorrow; but the bad news will turn to good.

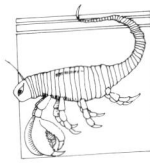

SCORPIO (Oct 24–Nov 22) You will make an unexpected journey, and you will find something very good at the end of it.

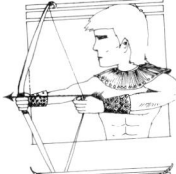

SAGITTARIUS (Nov 23–Dec 21) You will have trouble with a person who loves you; and you will have help from a person who doesn't.

CAPRICORN (Dec 22–Jan 20) A letter will bring a very great surprise, and some unhappiness, but a good friend will make things better.

1 Read your horoscope with a dictionary. Memorize it – and see if it comes true.

2 Work with some more people who have the same sign as you, if possible.
Write a new horoscope for your sign, and for another one.

3 Make some predictions about football matches. Examples:

'Arsenal will beat Liverpool 3 – 1 next Saturday.'

Or make predictions about some other sport. Or about the 'top twenty' records. Example:

'"Baby come here" will be number one.'
'"Get out of my heart" will go up three places.'

Remember your predictions and see if they come true.

4 How old will you be in the year 2000? What do you think you will be like? What about other people in the class? Write a few sentences about the future of yourself and some of the other students.

D A matter of life and death

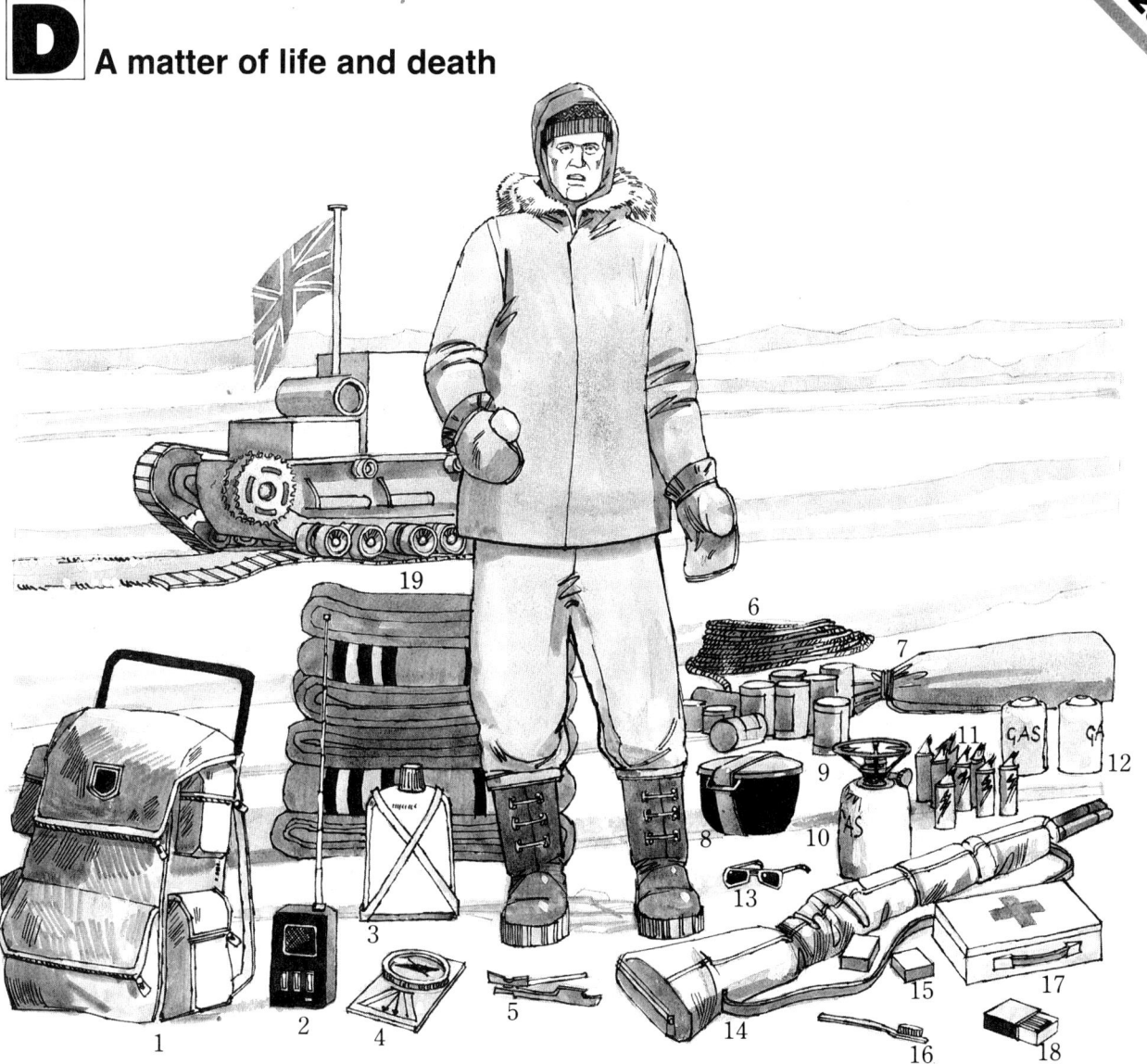

Unit 29D

1 You are at the North Pole. Your tractor and radio transmitter have broken down and you cannot repair them. You have to walk 100 miles (160 km) to the nearest camp. You have enough warm clothing and boots; you also have the following things on the tractor, but you can't carry them all. What will you take? Choose carefully – it's a matter of life and death.

matches (20g)
saucepan (500g)
large water bottle (empty 300g, full 2.5kg)
tent (4kg)
tin-opener (80g)
first aid kit (500g)
backpack (1.5kg)
sunglasses (40g)
gas cartridges (300g each)

ten blankets (1.5kg each)
gas cooker (1.2kg)
toothbrush (10g)
20m of rope (3kg)
compass (50g)
small radio receiver (1.2kg)
rifle and ammunition (6.9kg)
30kg of tinned food
ten signal flares (1.5kg)

2 Look at the summary on page 157 with your teacher.

Unit 30

Useful; useless

A All you need is love

1 Who needs what? Make some sentences.

People Men		people. men.
Women Babies	need	women. babies. fish.
Fish Cars	don't need	bicycles. cars. milk.
Animals Gardens		love. freedom. water.
		petrol. oil. sleep.
		politicians. books.
		clothes.

2 What do people need in life? Make a list of ten things. You can use your dictionary. What do *you* need now?

3 How important are these things to you? Very important? Quite important? Not very important?
Which is the most important? Which is the least important? List them in order of importance, and compare lists with three other students.

a car	children	TV	interesting work
money	love	freedom	nice clothes
music	friends	books	time to be alone

4 We asked some people to name two things each that were very important to them. Which ten different things do you think they named?

family	home	life	freedom	car
friends	friendship	music	happiness	
money	rugby boots	work	health	

Now listen, and see if you were right. Try to note how many times each thing is named as important.

5 Listen to the short extracts from songs, and try to write the words.

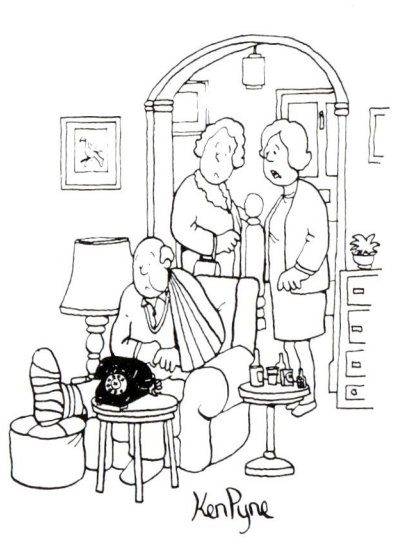

"He's got toothache, a sprained ankle, a bad back, gout, influenza, a broken arm and an ulcer and he's just hoping someone will ring him up and ask him how he is."

B Is it useful?

1 Work in pairs. Which of these subjects are necessary for a good education? Which are useful? Which are useless? Make three lists to read to the class.

reading	spelling	mathematics	history
geography	sports	physical sciences	
literature	biology	religious education	
English	typing	cookery	

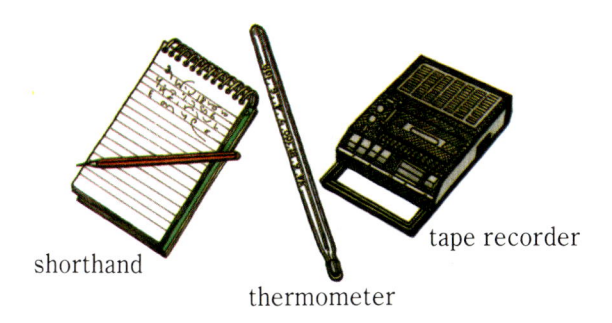

2 Work in groups. Choose four jobs and decide which school subjects are ✓✓ necessary ✓ useful ✗ useless for each one.

	Architect	Banker	Doctor	Engineer	Farmer	Journalist	Photographer	Secretary	Businessman or Businesswoman
Mathematics									
English									
Geography									
Latin									
History									
Typing									
Biology									
Art									
Physics									
Chemistry									

3 These people are beginning their last two years of school. They can each take five of the subjects from Exercise 2. Which five subjects should each one take? Why?

1. Pat wants to be a doctor. She enjoys languages.
2. John would like to be an architect. He does well in sciences, but they are not his favourite subjects.
3. Judy will own and manage the family farm when she is older. She likes to travel.
4. Tom plans to be a journalist. He would like to write about international politics.

4 Complete the sentences.

1. A photographer uses a camera to take pictures with.
2. A journalist uses a tape recorder to record interviews with.
3. ....
4. An architect .... drafting table .... draw plans on.
5. .... in.
6. .... tractors .... plough fields ....
7. ....
8. .... a barn .... keep cows ....

1. A photographer takes pictures with a camera.
2. ....
3. Farmers milk cows with milking machines.
4. ....
5. .... secretary takes notes in shorthand.
6. ....
7. Nurses take temperatures .... thermometers.
8. ....

shorthand

thermometer

tape recorder

tractor

field

barn

Unit 30C

C It's useless (part one)

ASSISTANT: Good afternoon, madam. Can I help you?
CUSTOMER: Yes, I'd like to see the manager, please.
ASSISTANT: Furniture, madam? Second floor.
CUSTOMER: No, the *manager. Ma-na-ger.*
ASSISTANT: Oh, I *am* sorry. I thought you said furniture.
CUSTOMER: That's all right. But can I see the manager, please?
ASSISTANT: Well, I'm afraid he's *very* busy just now. Have you an appointment?
CUSTOMER: No, I haven't. I want to make a complaint.
ASSISTANT: A complaint. Oh, I see. Well, I'll just see if he's free.

1 Listen to the conversation. Then decide whether these sentences are true or false.

1. The conversation happens in the afternoon.
2. The customer wants to buy furniture.
3. She is on the second floor.
4. The assistant doesn't understand what she wants.
5. The woman hasn't got an appointment.
6. The manager is not free.
7. The woman wants to complain about something.

2 Study the conversation, and practise it in pairs.

3 Work with a partner, and make up a short conversation which includes a misunderstanding and an apology. You can use one of these sentences if you like.

I thought you said Thursday.
I thought you said goodbye.
I thought you said five pence.
I thought you said five o'clock.
I thought you said steak.
I thought you were talking to me.

4 Stress. List each of these words under one of the stress patterns. Then pronounce them.

happiness   furniture   animal
bicycle   afternoon   literature
mathematics appointment

■ □ □   □ □ ■   ■ □ □
manager   *engineer*   *already*

D It's useless (part two)

MANAGER: Good afternoon, madam. I understand you have a complaint.
CUSTOMER: Yes, I've got a problem with this hair-drier.
MANAGER: I'm sorry to hear that. What's the trouble?
CUSTOMER: Well, first of all, I ordered it two months ago and it only arrived yesterday.
MANAGER: Oh dear. That's very strange.
CUSTOMER: Well, it's probably because you addressed it to Mr Paul Jones at 29 Cannon Street. I'm *Mrs Paula* Jones, and my address is *39* Cannon Street.
MANAGER: Well, I'm really sorry about that, madam. We do...
CUSTOMER: And secondly, I'm afraid it's useless. It doesn't work.
MANAGER: Doesn't work?
CUSTOMER: No. It doesn't work. It doesn't dry my hair. When I switch it on, it just goes 'bzzzzz', but it doesn't get hot at all.
MANAGER: Well, I really am very sorry about this, madam. I do apologize. We'll be happy to replace the drier for you. Or we'll give you a refund instead, if you prefer.
CUSTOMER: And thirdly, ...

1 Listen to the conversation. Find out what the new words and expressions mean.

2 Practise the conversation with a partner.

3 Stress. Listen carefully to these questions, and then write answers to them (beginning *No, ...*). When you have done that, practise saying the questions and answers.

1. You've got *two* sisters, haven't you?
   No, just one
2. You've got two *sisters*, haven't you?
   No, two brothers
3. You work in London, don't you?
4. Is that Mary's father?
5. Did you say you had a new red Lancia?
6. Do you need English for your work?

Now listen to this question. You will hear it three times, with three different stresses. Can you write suitable answers (a different answer each time)?

7. Would you like me to telephone Peter and Anne?

4 Many words in English can be used in different ways. For example, *rain* can be used as a noun (*Look at the rain!*), or as a verb (*It will rain tomorrow*); and *open* can be used as a verb (*Is it OK if I open the window?*) or an adjective (*the open door*). Can you find any words in the conversation that can be used in different ways like this? Can you think of any other words?

5 Which of these words can be used in more than one way?

| arrive | answer | orange | music | phone |
| cold | pub | hear | clean | bath | change | warm |

6 A *shop* that sells *shoes* is a *shoe shop* (not a ~~shoes shop~~). How can you say:

a *lamp* in the *street*
the *door* of a *garage*
a *wheel* of a *bicycle*
a *bottle* for *beer*
a *race* for *horses*
a *shop* that sells *books*
a *window* in a *kitchen*
a *horse* that runs in *races*
a *boy* who brings *newspapers*
a *finger* you put a *ring* on

7 Prepare and practise a sketch about a complaint.

8 Look at the summary on page 158 with your teacher.

125

Unit 31
Self and others

A Do it yourself

1 Work with two other people. Tell them to do things, like this:

> Look at   Sing to
> Touch   Talk about
> Talk to
> Shake hands with

> yourselves.
>
> each other.

a woman looking at herself in a mirror

a man looking at himself in a mirror

falling in love with each other ××

2 You can look at yourself, or you can look at somebody else.
You can talk to yourself or to somebody else.
Can you do all these things to somebody else *and* to yourself?

hurt   visit   fall in love with   photograph
marry   employ   teach   wash
think about   telephone

3 Draw small pictures for these situations.

He's looking at her.
She's looking at herself.
They're looking at each other.
He's not looking at her, he's looking at somebody else.

4 Alan bought six things yesterday – three for himself and three for somebody else. Which were which, do you think?

a bunch of roses   a bottle of perfume
a train ticket   a stamp
a cigar   a birthday card

5 Do you do these things yourself, or does somebody else do them for you? Examples:

1. 'I do the ironing myself.'
2. 'Somebody else does the decorating.'

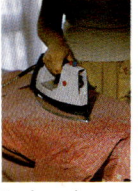

1. ironing   2. decorating   3. cooking   4. washing

5. cleaning   6. washing-up   7. shopping

Now listen to an English person answering the same questions.

6 Do you prefer to do these things by yourself or with somebody else?

listen to music   go to the cinema
go shopping   go on holiday
have lunch   go for a walk

126

B Shall I open it for you?

1 Put the sentences in the right pictures.

Shall I open it for you?	Shall I get it for you?
Shall I carry something for you?	I'll go, shall I?
Shall I have a look?	I'll answer it, shall I?

2 What do you think the answers will be?
Can you complete the sentences?

1. 'Can I take your coat?'
   'Oh, thank you. Here ....'
   'No, thanks. I'll keep .... on. I'm ....'

2. 'Shall I make you a cup of tea?'
   'Thank you very much. I'd love ....'
   'Not just now, thanks. I'm not ....'
   'I'd prefer coffee, if you've ....'

3. 'Would you like some toast?'
   'No, nothing ...., thanks.'
   'Yes, ... love .... Thank you.'
   'No, I've just ...., thanks.'

4. 'Would you like to go and see a film this evening?'
   'That would be very ....'
   'I'd love .... time?'
   'Not this evening, ... Perhaps .... time?'

5. 'Would you like to dance?'
   'Thanks. .... love ....'
   'Not .... now, thanks. I'm a bit ....'

6. 'Shall I help you to carry that?'
   'That's .... kind of you. Thank you.'
   'No, thanks. I can do it ....'

3 Prepare your answers to the following questions.
Then close your book, listen to the recording and answer.

Can I take your coat?
Shall I make you a cup of tea?
Would you like some toast?
Would you like to go and see a film this evening?
Shall I put the TV on?
Would you like a drink?
Would you like to have a rest?
Would you like to see my family photos?
Shall I telephone the station for you?
Would you like to wash your hands?

4 Prepare a conversation with another student (an offer and an answer). Act the conversation *without speaking*. The other students will try to decide what the words are.

5 Listen to the sentences. How many words do you hear? Write the first three words in each sentence. (Contractions like *that's* or *I'd* count as two words.)

127

Unit 31C

C Whose is that?

1 Match the pictures and the sentences.

> Mine, mine, all mine!   Is this yours?   It's his.
> Our baby's prettier than theirs.   Whose is that?
> My feet are smaller than hers.   At last! It's ours!

2 *His*, *hers* or *not sure*?

3 Exchange possessions with other students. Then ask '*Whose is this?*' See if everybody can remember.

4 Put in *my*, *mine*, *your*, *yours*, *his*, *her*, *hers*, *our*, *ours*, *their* or *theirs*.

1. 'Excuse me, that's .... coat.'
2. 'Oh, is it? I'm sorry – I thought it was ....'
3. We've got the same kind of house as Mr and Mrs Martin, but .... is a bit bigger than ours.
4. Could we have .... bill, please?
5. 'Is that Jane's cat?' 'No, this one's white. .... is black.'
6. 'Have you seen .... new motorbike?' 'Oh, it isn't .... He's just borrowed it.'
7. 'When's .... birthday?' 'December 15th.' 'Really? Mine's the day before ....'
8. Mary and .... boyfriend are taking .... holiday in June – the same time as we're taking .... Why don't we all go together?

5 Listen to the conversations and fill in the table.

	George	Keith	Pat	Edna	Jane
The car belongs to					
The new trousers belong to					
The glasses belong to					
The dictionary belongs to					
The plate belongs to					
The history book belongs to					

D Do you ever talk to yourself?

1 Survey of people's personal habits.
a. Make sure you know how to answer all the following questions in English.
b. Choose one of the questions (a different one from the other students), and go round the class asking the others your question.
c. Work out a statistic. Examples:

'Seventy-five per cent of the students in this class eat between meals.'
'Three students out of eight talk to themselves.'

1. Do you lie in bed after waking up?
2. Do you like people to talk to you before breakfast?
3. What do you have for breakfast?
4. Do you get dressed before or after breakfast?
5. What do you wear in bed?
6. Do you eat between meals?
7. Do you ever shut yourself in the bathroom to get away from people?
8. Do you ever talk to yourself?
9. Do you daydream at work?
10. Do you have arguments with other people in your head?
11. Are you more awake in the morning or the evening?
12. Do you sing in the bath?
13. Do you wash your clothes yourself, or does somebody else wash them for you?
14. Do you often cook for yourself?
15. Do you like shopping?
16. Do you do your ironing yourself, or does somebody else do it for you?
17. Do you eat in bed?
18. Do you like looking in a mirror?

2 Put in one of these words.

somebody	anybody	everybody	nobody
something	anything	everything	nothing
somewhere	anywhere	everywhere	nowhere

1. .... can speak all the languages in the world.
2. I think there's .... at the door.
3. 'Where are my keys?' 'I've seen them ...., but I can't remember where.'
4. Have you got .... to eat?
5. Does .... know where I put my glasses?
6. You can find Coca Cola ....
7. I need .... to read – have you got a paper?
8. I'm bored – there's .... to do.
9. .... needs love.
10. My wife and I always tell each other ....
11. 'Come and see a film with us.' 'I don't want to go ....'
12. 'Where can I find a good job with plenty of money and no work?' '............'

3 Vocabulary revision. Which word is different?
Can you find a word that names all the others?
Example:

sofa   chair   table   wall   bed
'Wall is different. The others are all furniture.'

1. tea   coffee   bread   milk
2. cooking   cleaning   ironing   dancing
3. green   big   blue   red
4. fair   blond   red   green   grey   dark
5. water   meat   bread   fish
6. car   sheep   train   bicycle
7. Aries   Taurus   Mars   Gemini
8. July   Christmas   March   January
9. book   letter   TV   newspaper
10. uncle   friend   sister   mother

4 Now listen to a little boy doing the same kind of exercise. Which word does he choose each time, and what is his reason?

1. horse   dog   book   cat
2. fish   lamb   beef   pork
3. apple   orange   pear   banana
4. knife   fork   cup   spoon
5. run   walk   chair   jump
6. TV   grass   flower   tree
7. shout   cry   laugh   sing
8. Mummy   Daddy   Mark   Granny
9. watch   calculator   shirt   camera

5 Look at the summary on page 159 with your teacher.

Unit 32 Revision and fluency practice

A You have to throw a six

1 Put the beginnings and ends together.

SOME OF THE RULES OF SNAKES AND LADDERS

In order to move,	you have to throw a dice.
Before starting,	you have to go down it.
If you come to a snake,	you have to go back four squares.
If you come to a ladder,	you have to throw a six.
If you throw a six,	you have to go up it.
If you land on an occupied square,	you have to miss a turn.
If you throw three sixes one after another,	you can have another throw.

2 Match the games and the rules.

You have to hit a ball over a net.
You have to kick a ball into a net.
You have to hit a ball into a small hole.
You have to capture a king.
You have to hit a ball and run.
You have to hit a ball into a net with a stick.

hockey
chess
football
golf
tennis
baseball

3

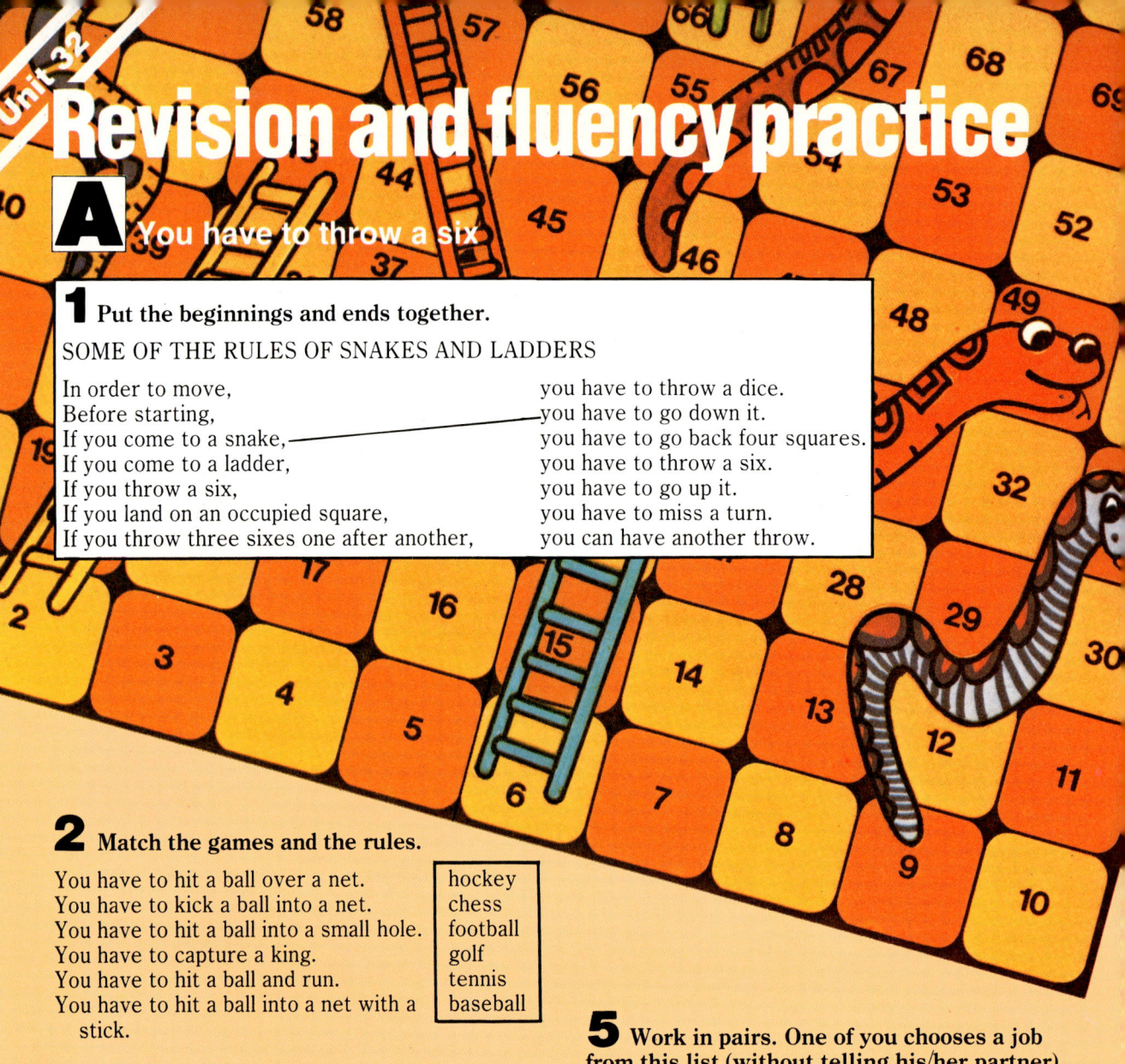

In Britain: nobody has to do military service; you don't have to carry an identity card; you have to drive on the left; you don't have to pay to go into a museum; you have to be over 18 to drink alcohol in a pub or bar; you have to pay for your drink before you drink it.
What is the situation in your country?

4 What do these people have to do?

A person who wants to travel by air.
A secretary.
Somebody who wants to cook a steak.
A person who wants to get into a university in your country.
A person who wants a driving licence.

5 Work in pairs. One of you chooses a job from this list (without telling his/her partner).

architect	lorry driver	coal miner	doctor
electrician	photographer	businessman	
secretary	pilot	teacher	shop assistant

The other asks the following questions, and then tries to guess his/her partner's job.

Do you have to get up early?
Do you have to get your hands dirty?
Do you have to travel?
Do you have to think a lot?
Do you have to study for a long time to learn the job?
Do you have to work long hours?
Do you have to handle money?
Do you have to work with people a lot?
Do you have to write letters?
Do you have to use machines?

B Get it right

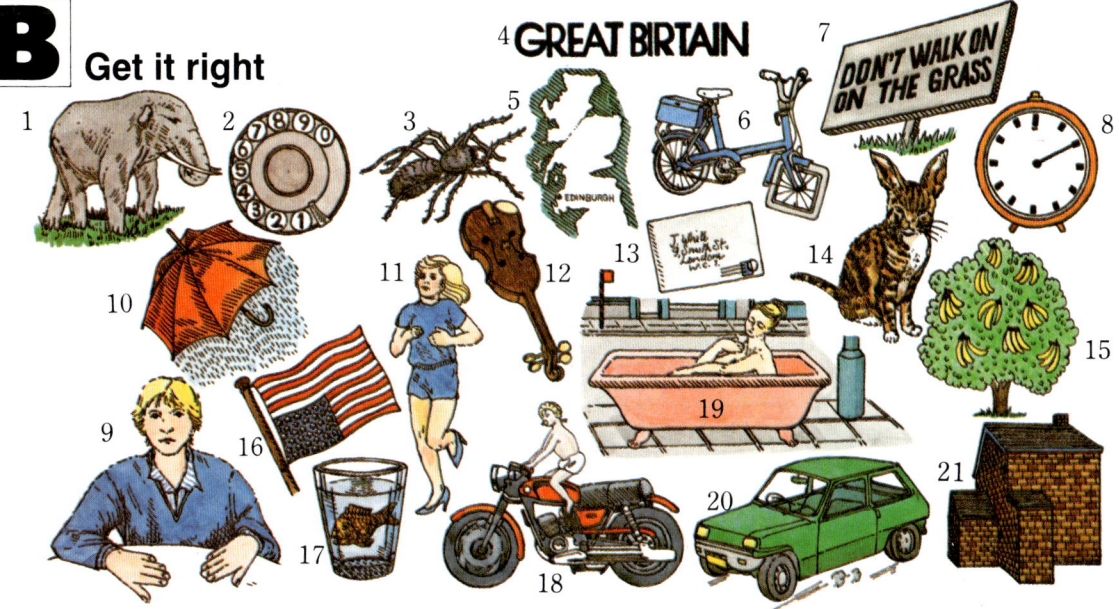

1 What's wrong with the pictures? Examples:

'The elephant's ears should be bigger.'
'The elephant's ears are too small.'

2 Put the parts of the story in the right order. Three of the parts don't belong in the story.

1. 'Excuse me,
2. and ordered a whisky.
3. and then he thought
4. so he stood up
5. The gorilla gave him the money
6. but he gave him the whisky,
7. A gorilla went into a pub,
8. There was silence for a few minutes,
9. 'Is it raining?'
10. so he asked him for £5.
11. but you don't often see a gorilla in a pub.'
12. and then the barman said
13. 'with whisky at £5 a glass.'
14. and started drinking.
15. 'It's not surprising,' said the gorilla
16. The barman was rather surprised,
17. on the other side of the room
18. 'Gorillas probably don't understand much about money,'
19. walked up to the bar,

3 In these sentences, some of the words are wrong. Listen to the recording and correct them.

1. 'Hello, Mary, I'm home,' said John, speaking rather fast.
2. 'John!' she said happily. 'Listen – a wonderful thing has happened.'
3. 'How's the car running?' 'Very well.'
4. 'Is your bath OK?' 'Just fine.'
5. 'Peter – how are you?' she said coldly.
6. Sally knocked at the door. 'Come in!' said a friendly voice.
7. It's a fine day. The sun's shining.
8. Little birds are singing.
9. Robert walked quietly up the stairs.

4 Put the correct verb form into the sentences.

1. I .... 800km yesterday. (drive)
2. We .... our cousins from Scotland last weekend. (see)
3. 'How was the party?' 'Very nice. George .... too much.' (drink)
4. That child .... too much TV. (watch)
5. I don't like .... (shop)
6. 'Would you like a cigarette?' 'No, thanks. ....' (I don't smoke / I'm not smoking)
7. What .... tomorrow? (do you do / are you doing)
8. 'Shall we go out?' 'No, ...' (it rains / it's raining)
9. I .... Mary for about six years. (know)
10. .... you ever .... Japanese food? (eat)

5 Make questions.

1. where | your wife | work?
2. your children | live | with you?
3. you ever | been | to Africa?
4. Mary and Peter | going to | get married?
5. What | your father | do | when he stops work next year?
6. why | you | come home so late last night?

131

Unit 32C

C Listening and cartoons

1 Listen to the song, and try to write down the words.

2 Listen to the story, and imagine or mime the actions.

3 Say what you think of the cartoons. Examples:

'I think number one's funny. I don't like number two.'
'I don't understand number three. I like number four best.'

1. "Bills, bills, bills..."

2.

3. MY SON IS INNOCENT

4. "I'M SURE YOU AND MOTHER WILL LIKE EACH OTHER."

5. 'Well, If I Called the Wrong Number, Why Did You Answer the Phone?'

D A visitor

Unit 32D

Prepare and practise a sketch with two or three other students. In your sketch, you must have:

A VISITOR

This can be a person, an animal, a thing... You decide.

A PROBLEM

For example:

Somebody is feeling ill.
There isn't enough money.
Somebody or something is lost.
Somebody can't understand.
Somebody is unhappy.
Something is broken.
Something doesn't work.

ROLES

Decide who you are.

What are your names?
What are your jobs?
What kind of personalities do you have?

'LANGUAGE FUNCTIONS'

Use English to do some of these things:

buy
sell
ask for information
explain
complain
invite
greet
suggest
order
offer
describe
compliment
compare
give instructions
express feelings
predict
borrow
lend
get to know somebody
give opinions
thank
apologize

A PLACE

Where are you? Perhaps:

at an airport
on a plane
on a ship
on a train
in a hotel
in a restaurant
in a shop
at a station
in a park
in the street
at home
in a pub
at the doctor's
at the North Pole
in the Sahara Desert
on the moon

SUMMARIES

Unit 23

Grammar and structures

Imperatives
Wear comfortable clothing.
Always **warm up**.
Never **run** in fog.
Don't run after a meal.

Don't run if you have a cold.

Prepositions of position and movement
Position: on, in, under, by
Movement: on, on to, in, into, under, by, off, out of

Instructions
Written instructions: Wash mushrooms and pat dry.
Spoken instructions: **You** wash **the** mushrooms and pat **them** dry.

It's on the chair. It **should be** on the table.

Words and expressions to learn

Nouns
advice /əd'vaɪs/ (uncountable)
a cold /ə 'kəʊld/
picture /'pɪktʃə(r)/
floor /flɔ:(r)/

Learn six or more of these:
lemon /'lemən/
pepper /'pepə(r)/
salt /sɔ:lt/
juice /dʒu:s/
fork /fɔ:k/
tablespoon /'teɪblspu:n/
bowl /bəʊl/
oil /ɔɪl/
cloth /klɒθ/
frying pan /'fraɪɪŋ 'pæn/
saucepan /'sɔ:spən/

Verbs
hurry /'hʌri/ (hurried, hurried)
worry /'wʌri/ (worried, worried)
wait /weɪt/
follow /'fɒləʊ/
drop /drɒp/ (dropped, dropped)
pick up /pɪk 'ʌp/
throw /θrəʊ/ (threw /θru:/, thrown /θrəʊn/)
throw away /θrəʊ ə'weɪ/
put away /pʊt ə'weɪ/
rest /rest/
should /ʃʊd/

Learn one or more of these:
fry /fraɪ/
slice /slaɪs/
mix /mɪks/
pour /pɔ:(r)/

Other words and expressions
before /bɪ'fɔ:(r)/
into /'ɪntə/
off /ɒf/
fresh /freʃ/
alone /ə'ləʊn/
most of /'məʊst əv/
early /'ɜ:li/
away /ə'weɪ/
after (conjunction) /'ɑ:ftə(r)/
Look out. /lʊk 'aʊt/
Be careful. /bi: 'keəfl/
take (your) time /'teɪk (jə) 'taɪm/

Unit 24

Grammar and structures

a dollar		night
57 pence	**a**	kilo
an apple		day

To get from Oxford Circus to Paddington, you **have to** change twice.

You can get from Bond Street to Leicester Square **without changing**.

153

Words and expressions to learn

Nouns
credit card /'kredɪt kɑːd/
cash /kæʃ/
shower /ʃaʊə(r)/
form /fɔːm/
stop /stɒp/
line /laɪn/
way /weɪ/
boarding pass /'bɔːdɪŋ pɑːs/
gate /geɪt/
flight /flaɪt/
arrival /ə'raɪvl/
departure /dɪ'pɑːtʃə/
reservation /rezə'veɪʃn/
hand baggage /'hænd 'bægɪdʒ/
timetable /'taɪmteɪbl/
air /eə(r)/
airport /'eəpɔːt/

airline /'eəlaɪn/
side /saɪd/
crossroads /'krɒsrəʊdz/
bridge /brɪdʒ/
river /'rɪvə(r)/

Verbs
get to /'get tə, 'get tuː/
pay /peɪ/ (paid /peɪd/, paid /peɪd/)
check in /tʃek 'ɪn/
fill in /fɪl 'ɪn/
have to /'hæftə, 'hæftuː/

Other words and expressions
including /ɪŋ'kluːdɪŋ/
over /'əʊvə(r)/
along /ə'lɒŋ/
on to /'ɒntə, 'ɒntʊ/
by credit card
by cheque
in cash
on the way
by air
double room /'dʌbl 'ruːm/

Unit 25

Grammar and structures

Going to
I'm **going to write** letters this evening.
This is **going to be** my room.
She's **going to have** a baby.
What are all your friends **going to do** when they leave school?

'Why did you come here?' '**To see** you.' (For to see you.)

Infinitives and *-ing* forms
Infinitive without to: I can **swim**.
Infinitive with to: Would you like **to dance**?
-ing form: Do you like **dancing**?
(For details, see Lesson 25D.)

Words and expressions to learn

Nouns
plan /plæn/
country /'kʌntri/
cost /kɒst/
details /'diːteɪlz/
library /'laɪbri/
butcher's /'bʊtʃəz/
embassy /'embəsi/
travel agent /'trævl 'eɪdʒənt/
information /ɪnfə'meɪʃn/
visa /'viːzə/
suitcase /'suːtkeɪs/
aeroplane /'eərəpleɪn/
air ticket /'eə tɪkɪt/
baby /'beɪbi/

Verbs
study /'stʌdi/
win /wɪn/ (won /wʌn/, won /wʌn/)
crash /kræʃ/
organize /'ɔːgənaɪz/
join /dʒɔɪn/

Other words and expressions
fit /fɪt/
inclusive /ɪŋ'kluːsɪv/
hard work /'hɑːd 'wɜːk/
have a baby /'hæv ə 'beɪbi/
first of all /'fɜːst əv 'ɔːl/
not yet /nɒt 'jet/
play cards /pleɪ 'kɑːdz/

154

Unit 26

Grammar and structures

Feelings

| It | depresses / frightens | me. | | It makes me | angry. / happy. / unhappy. | | He gets | angry / worried / bored | when he goes there. |

-ed and -ing

Does this **interest** you? It **interests** me. I'm **interested** in it. It's **interesting**. (~~I'm interesting in it.~~)
Does John **bore** you? He **bores** me. I'm **bored**. He's **boring**. (~~I'm boring by him.~~)

| easy / nice / difficult | to | talk **to** / work **with** / see etc. |

Words and expressions to learn

Nouns
flu /fluː/ (uncountable)
a temperature /ə 'temprɪtʃə(r)/ (countable)
headache /'hedeɪk/ (countable)
toothache /'tuːθeɪk/ (uncountable)
aspirin /'æsprɪn/
medicine /'medsən/
matter /'mætə(r)/
dinner /'dɪnə(r)/
pleasure /'pleʒə(r)/
freedom /'friːdəm/
mistake /mɪs'teɪk/
marriage /'mærɪdʒ/
couple /'kʌpl/

Verbs
feel /fiːl/ (felt /felt/, felt /felt/)
hurt /hɜːt/ (hurt /hɜːt/, hurt /hɜːt/)
frighten /'fraɪtn/
depress /dɪ'pres/
disgust /dɪs'gʌst/
solve /sɒlv/
trust /trʌst/
get on (with) /get 'ɒn (wɪð)/
can't stand /kaːnt 'stænd/
appreciate /ə'priːʃieɪt/
share /ʃeə(r)/
lie down /laɪ 'daʊn/
  (lay /leɪ/, lain /leɪn/)

Adjectives
ill /ɪl/
angry /'æŋgri/
fed up /'fed 'ʌp/
fair /feə(r)/

Other words and expressions
That's very nice of you.
on the whole /ɒn ðə 'həʊl/
take medicine /'teɪk 'medsən/
What's the matter?
change (my) mind
  /'tʃeɪndʒ (maɪ) 'maɪnd/

Unit 27

Grammar and structures

Get

Get + **noun** = *receive, obtain, fetch* etc.
  get a letter   get a drink

Get + **adverb particle/preposition** = *move*
  get up   get into a car

Get + **adjective** = *become*
  It's getting cold.

Have got
  I've got two brothers.

Adverbs of manner

She speaks English **well**. (~~She speaks well English.~~)
I like skiing **very much**. (~~I like very much skiing.~~)

slow – slow**ly**
careful – careful**ly**
nice – nice**ly**

happy – happ**ily**
comforta**ble** – comforta**bly**

155

Words and expressions to learn

Nouns
boat /bəʊt/
motorbike /'məʊtəbaɪk/
taxi /'tæksi/
bus /bʌs/
journey /'dʒɜːni/
lightning /'laɪtnɪŋ/
race /reɪs/
speed /spiːd/
record /'rekɔːd/
button /'bʌtn/
handle /'hændl/
packet /'pækɪt/
flower /'flaʊə(r)/
second /'sekənd/

Verbs
ride /raɪd/ (rode /rəʊd/, ridden /'rɪdn/)
fly /flaɪ/ (flew /fluː/, flown /fləʊn/)
hitchhike /'hɪtʃhaɪk/
guess /ges/
press /pres/
pull /pʊl/
push /pʊʃ/
turn /tɜːn/
get on /get 'ɒn/
get off /get 'ɒf/
get in(to) /get 'ɪn(tə)/
get out (of) /get 'aʊt (əv)/
breathe /briːð/

Adjectives
electric /ɪ'lektrɪk/
sleepy /'sliːpi/
thin /θɪn/

Adverbs
sleepily /'sliːpəli/
happily /'hæpəli/
kindly /'kaɪndli/
angrily /'æŋgrəli/
loudly /'laʊdli/
quietly /'kwaɪətli/
coldly /'kəʊldli/
shyly /'ʃaɪli/
noisily /'nɔɪzəli/
badly /'bædli/
nicely /'naɪsli/
comfortably /'kʌmftəbli/

Other words and expressions
by plane /baɪ 'pleɪn/
by boat /baɪ 'bəʊt/
one day /wʌn 'deɪ/
like lightning /laɪk 'laɪtnɪŋ/

Summary Unit 28

Grammar and structures

Quantifiers
Very few pupils go to private schools.
Not many pupils...
Some pupils...
Two thirds of American pupils...
Three quarters of...
Most pupils...
Nearly all pupils...
More British pupils... than American pupils...
Far more pupils...
75% of American pupils...
Less than 5% of British pupils...

Fractions
⅔ two thirds
¾ three quarters
⅞ seven eighths
3/20 three twentieths

Prepositions
at the top   **at** the bottom
at the beginning   **at** the end
in the middle
at 16 (years old)

Structuring paragraphs
First...   Next...   Then...   After that...   Finally...

Words and expressions to learn

Nouns
private school /'praɪvɪt 'skuːl/
state school /'steɪt 'skuːl/
country /'kʌntri/
top /tɒp/
bottom /'bɒtəm/
front /frʌnt/
back /bæk/
corner /'kɔːnə(r)/
middle /'mɪdl/
circle /'sɜːkl/
cross /krɒs/
square /skweə(r)/
triangle /'traɪæŋgl/
beginning /bɪ'gɪnɪŋ/
end /end/
soup /suːp/
theatre /'θɪətə(r)/
zoo /zuː/
policeman /pə'liːsmən/
map /mæp/

Verbs
shave /ʃeɪv/
wash /wɒʃ/
get dressed /get 'drest/
put on (clothes) /pʊt 'ɒn/
take off (clothes) /teɪk 'ɒf/
brush (teeth, hair) /brʌʃ/
go out (lights etc.) /gəʊ 'aʊt/
ring (phone) /rɪŋ/ (rang/ræŋ/, rung/rʌŋ/)

Other words and expressions
far more /'fɑ: 'mɔ:(r)/
most /məʊst/
less /les/
nearly /'nɪəli/
true /tru:/
inside /ɪn'saɪd/
outside /aʊt'saɪd/
What else? /wɒt 'els/

Unit 29

Grammar and structures

Future: *will*

I will start	I'll start
you will start	you'll start
he/she/it will start	he'll/she'll/it'll start
we will start	we'll start
they will start	they'll start

will I start?	I will not start	I won't start
will you start?	you will not start	you won't start
etc.	etc.	etc.

I'll take money with me.
You'll get lost. No, I **won't**.
You **won't** get lifts. Yes, I **will**.

Get
You'll **get** lost. You'll **get** killed.
I'm going to **get** married.

Words and expressions to learn

Nouns

Learn six or more of these:
word /wɜ:d/
death /deθ/
heart /hɑ:t/
lover /'lʌvə(r)/
youth hostel /'ju:θ hɒstl/
prison /'prɪzn/
pilot /'paɪlət/
decision /dɪ'sɪʒən/
trouble /'trʌbl/
accident /'æksɪdənt/
opportunity /ɒpə'tju:nəti/
news /nju:z/
star /stɑ:(r)/
misunderstanding
 /mɪsʌndə'stændɪŋ/

Learn six or more of these:
tractor /'træktə(r)/
rope /rəʊp/
bottle /'bɒtl/
blanket /'blæŋkɪt/
tent /tent/
gas /gæs/
sunglasses /'sʌnglɑ:sɪz/
matches /'mætʃɪz/
tin /tɪn/
tin-opener /'tɪn'əʊpnə(r)/
toothbrush /'tu:θbrʌʃ/
rifle /'raɪfl/
compass /'kʌmpəs/
backpack /'bækpæk/

Verbs
get lost /get 'lɒst/
get married /get 'mærɪd/
enjoy /ɪn'dʒɔɪ/
won't /wəʊnt/
dream /dri:m/
pass /pɑ:s/
fall in love /fɔ:l ɪn 'lʌv/

Adjectives
dangerous /'deɪndʒərəs/
dead /ded/
tinned /tɪnd/
famous /'feɪməs/

Preposition
round /raʊnd/

Summary Unit 30

Grammar and structures

Use
A farmer uses a barn to keep cows in.　　A farmer keeps cows in a barn.
Nurses use thermometers to take temperatures with.　　Nurses take temperatures with thermometers.
You use a wallet to keep money in.　　You keep money in a wallet.
You use a key to open a door with.　　You open a door with a key.

Stress
'You've got *two* sisters, haven't you?' 'No, just one.'
'You've got two *sisters*, haven't you?' 'No, two brothers.'

Words having different functions

Verb	Noun	Adjective
1. **Phone** me at 7.00.	1. a blue **phone**	1. –
2. Could you **bath** the baby?	2. He's having a **bath**.	2. –
3. **Open** your mouth and say 'Ah'.	3. –	3. The door was partly **open**.
4. It doesn't **dry** my hair.	4. –	4. It was a very **dry** day.
5. –	5. Have an **orange**.	5. an **orange** car

Nouns used a little like adjectives
a **box** with a **phone** in it = a phone box
a **shop** that sells **books** = a book shop (a books shop)
a **wheel** of a **bicycle** = a bicycle wheel
a **race** for **horses** = a horse race

Words and expressions to learn

Nouns
garden /'gɑːdn/
petrol /'petrʊl/
oil /ɔɪl/
complaint /kəm'pleɪnt/
appointment /ə'pɔɪntmənt/
customer /'kʌstəmə(r)/

Learn six or more of these:
mathematics /mæθ'mætɪks/
history /'hɪstəri/
geography /dʒi'ɒgrəfi/
spelling /'spelɪŋ/
literature /'lɪtrətʃə(r)/
science /'saɪəns/
biology /baɪ'ɒlədʒi/
religion /rɪ'lɪdʒən/
cookery /'kʊkəri/
art /ɑːt/
physics /'fɪzɪks/
chemistry /'kemɪstri/
banker /'bæŋkə(r)/
farmer /'fɑːmə(r)/
journalist /'dʒɜːnəlɪst/
happiness /'hæpɪnəs/
friendship /'frendʃɪp/
health /helθ/
refund /'riːfʌnd/

Verbs
order /'ɔːdə(r)/
switch on /swɪtʃ 'ɒn/
switch off /swɪtʃ 'ɒf/
(It doesn't) work
go (bzzz)
apologize /ə'pɒlədʒaɪz/
replace /rɪ'pleɪs/
prefer /prɪ'fɜː(r)/

Adjectives
useless /'juːsləs/
necessary /'nesəsri/
busy /'bɪzi/
strange /streɪndʒ/

Other words and expressions
least /liːst/
That's all right.
I thought you said...
secondly /'sekəndli/
thirdly /'θɜːdli/
I *do* apologize. /aɪ 'duː ə'pɒlədʒaɪz/
instead /ɪn'sted/

Unit 31

Grammar and structures

Reflexive pronouns

| myself /maɪˈself/ |
| yourself /jɔːˈself/ |
| himself /hɪmˈself/ |
| herself /həˈself/ |
| itself /ɪtˈself/ |
| ourselves /aʊəˈselvz/ |
| yourselves /jɔːˈselvz/ |
| themselves /ðəmˈselvz/ |

Stop looking at **yourself** in the mirror.
'Can I help you?' 'I'll do it **myself**, thanks.'
I like going for walks **by myself**.

Possessive pronouns

| mine /maɪn/ |
| yours /jɔːz/ |
| his /hɪz/ |
| hers /hɜːz/ |
| ours /aʊəz/ |
| theirs /ðeəz/ |

That's not **yours** – it's **mine**.
Our baby's prettier than **theirs**.

Whose is that?

Indefinite pronouns

somebody	anybody	everybody	nobody
something	anything	everything	nothing
somewhere	anywhere	everywhere	nowhere

There's **somebody** at the door.
Would you like **anything** to drink?
You can find Coca Cola **everywhere**.
'What are you doing?' '**Nothing**.'

Shall

Shall I carry something for you?
I'll open the door, **shall** I?

Would

Would you like something to drink?
I'd like some tea.
I'd prefer coffee.
'**Would** you like to dance?' 'I'd love to.'

Else

Do you do the ironing yourself, or does **somebody else** do it for you?
'Would you like **something else**?' 'No, **nothing else**, thank you.'

Other structures

They talk to **each other** in English.
They've known **each other** for years.

do the ironing   do the cleaning   do the shopping

I've **just** had breakfast.

'Shall I take your coat?' 'No thanks, **I'll keep it on**.'

That's very kind of you.

That car belongs to my boss.

Words and expressions to learn

Nouns

the ironing /ði ˈaɪənɪŋ/
the cleaning /ðə ˈkliːnɪŋ/
the washing /ðə ˈwɒʃɪŋ/
the washing-up /ðə wɒʃɪŋ ˈʌp/
the shopping /ðə ˈʃɒpɪŋ/
toast /təʊst/
plate /pleɪt/
argument /ˈɑːgjʊmənt/
mirror /ˈmɪrə(r)/

Verbs

hurt /hɜːt/ (hurt /hɜːt/, hurt /hɜːt/)
visit /ˈvɪzɪt/
teach /tiːtʃ/ (taught /tɔːt/, taught /tɔːt/)
shall /ʃəl, ʃæl/
carry /ˈkæri/
put on (TV) /pʊt ˈɒn/
keep on (clothes) /kiːp ˈɒn/ (kept /kept/, kept /kept/)
belong (to) /bɪˈlɒŋ tə/
shut /ʃʌt/ (shut /ʃʌt/, shut /ʃʌt/)

Other words and expressions

about /əˈbaʊt/
else /els/
just /dʒʌst/
just now /dʒʌst ˈnaʊ/
whose /huːz/
awake /əˈweɪk/
anybody /ˈenibɒdi/
anywhere /ˈeniweə(r)/
nowhere /ˈnəʊweə(r)/
shake hands with /ʃeɪk ˈhændz wɪð/
get away from /get əˈweɪ frəm/
have a look /hæv ə ˈlʊk/
have a rest /hæv ə ˈrest/
wash (your) hands /wɒʃ (jɔː) ˈhændz/

THERE IS NO SUMMARY FOR UNIT 32.

Acknowledgements

The authors and publishers would like to thank the following institutions for their help in testing the material and for the invaluable feedback which they provided:

ILC, Paris, France; Sociedade Brasileira de Cultura Inglesa, Curitiba, Brazil; International Language Centre, Athens, Greece; Adult Migrant Education Service, Australia; Ecole Nationale des Ponts et Chaussées, Paris, France; Communications in Business, Paris, France; Audiovisuelles Sprachinstitut, Zürich, Switzerland; Institut Supérieur de Langues Vivantes, University of Liège, Belgium; Studio School of English, Cambridge; The Cambridge School of English, London; English International, London; International Language Centre, Kuwait; Instituto Anglo-Mexicano de Cultura, Mexico; The British Institute of Rome, Italy; Englisches Institut, Köln, West Germany; The Gulf Polytechnic, Bahrain; Institut de Linguistique Appliquée, Strasbourg; Université Lyon 2, France; Abteilung für Angewandte Linguistik, Universität Bern, Switzerland; The British Council, Milan, Italy; International House, Hastings; English Language Centre, Hove, Sussex; Newnham Language Centre, Cambridge; The British Centre, Venice, Italy; Glostrup Pædagogisk Central, Denmark; Kochi Women's University, Kochi-shi, Japan; Institut Français de Gestion, Paris, France; The British Institute, Paris, France; The British School, Florence, Italy; Helmonds Avondcollege, Netherlands; Kodak Pathé, Paris, France; Bell School, Cambridge; Oxford Language Centre, Oxford.

The authors and publishers are grateful to the following copyright owners for permission to reproduce photographs, illustrations, texts and music:

page 26: *tl* The Tate Gallery, London; *c* Reprinted by permission of Ekdotike Athenon, S.A.; *tr* Reprinted by permission of Royal Gallery of Paintings: Mauritshuis; *br* Copyright © Trustees of the British Museum. The excerpt on the cassette from *Eine Kleine Nachtmusik* by Mozart is from a Decca recording and is used with permission.   page 29: *bl* Copyright © 1954 by Ronald Searle; *br* Copyright © Associated Newspapers Group plc.   page 41: *br* Copyright © 1956 by Ronald Searle.   page 51: *t* Ms.Auct.D.inf.2.11, Folios 3,7 & 10 recto. By permission of The Bodleian Library, Oxford.   page 53: *c,cr* Copyright © Associated Newspapers Group plc; *br* Reproduced by permission of *Punch*.   page 61: Reproduced by permission of *Punch*.   page 65: *Musical Swag* by Pierre Ranson, Copyright © Tony Bingham.   page 80: *tr, bl* Reproduced by permission of *Punch*.   page 86: The words of *Why, Oh Why* are copyright © 1960, 1964 and 1972 Ludlow Music Inc. New York, assigned to Tro Essex Music Limited at 85 Gower Street, London WC1. International copyright secured. All rights reserved. Used by permission.   page 88: By permission of Rolls-Royce Motors Limited.   page 90: *l* Courtesy of the Prado Museum, Madrid; *r* Cliché des Musées Nationaux, Paris.   page 96: The lyrics of *Pick it up* are copyright © 1954 Folkways Music Publishers Inc. New York, assigned to Kensington Music Limited at 85 Gower Street, London WC1. International copyright secured. All rights reserved. Used by permission.   page 97: *t* copyright © Penguin Books 1973.   page 98: *br*, Courtesy of Hilton International, London.   page 99: *t* Reproduced by permission of London Transport (Registered User No. 83/200).   page 100: *c* Courtesy of British Airways.   page 117: *t* Reproduced by permission of *Punch*.   page 122: Reproduced by permission of *Punch*.   page 126: *ct, tr* By Lucy Bowden.   page 130: *t* Copyright © Garsmanda Limited.   page 132: *tl, tr, c* Reproduced by permission of *Punch*; *bl* Reproduced by permission of Express Newspapers; *br* From *The Thurber Carnival* by James Thurber. © 1943 James Thurber © 1963 Hamish Hamilton Limited. © 1971 Helen W. Thurber and Rosemary T. Sauers. From *Men, Women and Dogs* published by Harcourt Brace Jovanovich.

BBC Hulton Picture Library: p63 *cr, br*.   Brenard Photo Services Limited: p79.   Colorific Photo Library Limited: p7 *no. 4*, p19 *ct*, inset *bl, cr*, p21, p38 *cr*, p63 *cl*, p107 *nos. 1, 3, 5, 6*.   Colour Library International (Keystone Press Agency Limited): p7 *no. 3*, p9 *no. 2*, p107 *no. 2*, p109 *c*.   Daily Telegraph Colour Library: p19 inset *cl*.   The Image Bank of Photography: p66 *Thomas, Mike*, p67 *c B, D, F*, p109 *B, D, E, F*.   Alan Philip: p10 *nos. 1-6*, p17, p30 *t*, p35, p50 *r*, p71 *t*, p104 *t*, p115 *t*, p126 *br*.   Pictor International Limited: p9 *cr*, p11 *cr*, p14, p66 *Kate, Stuart, Ann*, p67 *A-E, c A, C, E*, p108 *cl, br*, p109 *A*.   Scala Istituto Fotografico Editoriale s.p.a: p63 *t*.   Sporting Pictures (UK) Limited: p78   Stockphotos International: p66 *Mark*, p107 *no.4*.   Tony Stone Associates: p19 *cr*, p108 *tr*.   Syndication International Limited: p7 *nos. 1, 5, 7, 8, 9*, p9 *nos. 5, 6*.   John Topham Picture Library: p7 *nos. 2, 6, 10*, p9 *nos. 1, 3, 4, 7, 8*, p19 *tl, ct, cb*, inset *tr, br*, p38 *tr*.

John Craddock: Malcolm Barter, Suzanne Lihou, Alexa Rutherford, Kate Simunek.   Ian Fleming and Associates Limited: Terry Burton.   Davis Lewis Management: Richard Dunn, Bob Harvey, Barry Thorpe.   Linden Artists Limited: David Astin, Jon Davies, Tim Marwood, Val Sangster, Malcolm Stokes, Linda Worrell.   Temple Art Agency: Mark Bergin, John James, John Marshall, Alan Philpot, Mike Whittlesea.   Richard Baldwin, Richard Child, Kaye Hodges, Chris Rawlings, Malcolm Ward, Mike Woodhatch, Youé and Spooner.

(*t* = top *b* = bottom *c* = centre *r* = right *l* = left)

Phonetic symbols

Vowels

symbol	example
/i:/	eat /i:t/
/i/	happy /ˈhæpi/
/ɪ/	it /ɪt/
/e/	when /wen/
/æ/	cat /kæt/
/ɑ:/	hard /hɑ:d/
/ɒ/	not /nɒt/
/ɔ:/	sort /sɔ:t/; all /ɔ:l/
/ʊ/	look /lʊk/
/u:/	too /tu:/
/ʌ/	up /ʌp/
/ɜ:/	bird /bɜ:d/; turn /tɜ:n/
/ə/	about /əˈbaʊt/; mother /ˈmʌðə(r)/
/eɪ/	day /deɪ/
/aɪ/	my /maɪ/
/ɔɪ/	boy /bɔɪ/
/aʊ/	now /naʊ/
/əʊ/	go /gəʊ/
/ɪə/	here /hɪə(r)/
/eə/	chair /tʃeə(r)/
/ʊə/	tour /tʊə(r)/

Consonants

symbol	example
/p/	pen /pen/
/b/	big /bɪg/
/t/	two /tu:/
/d/	do /du:/
/k/	look /lʊk/; cup /kʌp/
/g/	get /get/
/tʃ/	China /ˈtʃaɪnə/
/dʒ/	Japan /dʒəˈpæn/
/f/	fall /fɔ:l/
/v/	very /ˈveri/
/θ/	think /θɪŋk/
/ð/	then /ðen/
/s/	see /si:/
/z/	zoo /zu:/; is /ɪz/
/ʃ/	shoe /ʃu:/
/ʒ/	pleasure /ˈpleʒə(r)/; decision /dɪˈsɪʒn/
/h/	who /hu:/; how /haʊ/
/m/	meet /mi:t/
/n/	no /nəʊ/
/ŋ/	sing /sɪŋ/
/l/	long /lɒŋ/
/r/	right /raɪt/
/j/	yet /jet/
/w/	will /wɪl/

Stress

Stress is shown by a mark (ˈ) in front of the stressed syllable.

mother /ˈmʌðə(r)/ **Chi**na /ˈtʃaɪnə/
a**bout** /əˈbaʊt/ Ja**pan** /dʒəˈpæn/

Irregular verbs

Infinitive	Simple Past	Past Participle
be /bi:/	was /wəz, wɒz/; were /wə, wɜ:(r)/	been /bɪn, bi:n/
become /bɪˈkʌm/	became /bɪˈkeɪm/	become /bɪˈkʌm/
begin /bɪˈgɪn/	began /bɪˈgæn/	begun /bɪˈgʌn/
break /breɪk/	broke /brəʊk/	broken /ˈbrəʊkn/
bring /brɪŋ/	brought /brɔ:t/	brought /brɔ:t/
build /bɪld/	built /bɪlt/	built /bɪlt/
buy /baɪ/	bought /bɔ:t/	bought /bɔ:t/
catch /kætʃ/	caught /kɔ:t/	caught /kɔ:t/
come /kʌm/	came /keɪm/	come /kʌm/
cost /kɒst/	cost /kɒst/	cost /kɒst/
do /du, də, du:/	did /dɪd/	done /dʌn/
draw /drɔ:/	drew /dru:/	drawn /drɔ:n/
dream /dri:m/	dreamt /dremt/	dreamt /dremt/
drink /drɪŋk/	drank /dræŋk/	drunk /drʌŋk/
drive /draɪv/	drove /drəʊv/	driven /ˈdrɪvn/
eat /i:t/	ate /et/	eaten /ˈi:tn/
fall /fɔ:l/	fell /fel/	fallen /ˈfɔ:lən/
feel /fi:l/	felt /felt/	felt /felt/
find /faɪnd/	found /faʊnd/	found /faʊnd/
fly /flaɪ/	flew /flu:/	flown /fləʊn/
forget /fəˈget/	forgot /fəˈgɒt/	forgotten /fəˈgɒtn/
get /get/	got /gɒt/	got /gɒt/
give /gɪv/	gave /geɪv/	given /ˈgɪvn/
go /gəʊ/	went /went/	gone /gɒn/ been /bɪn, bi:n/
have /həv, hæv/	had /(h)əd, hæd/	had /hæd/
hear /hɪə(r)/	heard /hɜ:d/	heard /hɜ:d/
hurt /hɜ:t/	hurt /hɜ:t/	hurt /hɜ:t/
know /nju:/	knew /nju:/	known /nəʊn/
learn /lɜ:n/	learnt /lɜ:nt/	learnt /lɜ:nt/
leave /li:v/	left /left/	left /left/
lend /lend/	lent /lent/	lent /lent/
let /let/	let /let/	let /let/
lie /laɪ/	lay /leɪ/	lain /leɪn/
lose /lu:z/	lost /lɒst/	lost /lɒst/
make /meɪk/	made /meɪd/	made /meɪd/
mean /mi:n/	meant /ment/	meant /ment/
meet /mi:t/	met /met/	met /met/
pay /peɪ/	paid /peɪd/	paid /peɪd/
put /pʊt/	put /pʊt/	put /pʊt/
read /ri:d/	read /red/	read /red/
ride /raɪd/	rode /rəʊd/	ridden /ˈrɪdn/
ring /rɪŋ/	rang /ræŋ/	rung /rʌŋ/
rise /raɪz/	rose /rəʊz/	risen /ˈrɪzn/
run /rʌn/	ran /ræn/	run /rʌn/
say /seɪ/	said /sed/	said /sed/
see /si:/	saw /sɔ:/	seen /si:n/
sell /sel/	sold /səʊld/	sold /səʊld/
send /send/	sent /sent/	sent /sent/
shake /ʃeɪk/	shook /ʃʊk/	shaken /ˈʃeɪkn/
show /ʃəʊ/	showed /ʃəʊd/	shown /ʃəʊn/
shut /ʃʌt/	shut /ʃʌt/	shut /ʃʌt/
sing /sɪŋ/	sang /sæŋ/	sung /sʌŋ/
sit /sɪt/	sat /sæt/	sat /sæt/
sleep /sli:p/	slept /slept/	slept /slept/
speak /spi:k/	spoke /spəʊk/	spoken /ˈspəʊkn/
spell /spel/	spelt /spelt/	spelt /spelt/
spend /spend/	spent /spent/	spent /spent/
stand /stænd/	stood /stʊd/	stood /stʊd/
swim /swɪm/	swam /swæm/	swum /swʌm/
take /teɪk/	took /tʊk/	taken /ˈteɪkn/
teach /ti:tʃ/	taught /tɔ:t/	taught /tɔ:t/
tell /tel/	told /təʊld/	told /təʊld/
think /θɪŋk/	thought /θɔ:t/	thought /θɔ:t/
throw /θrəʊ/	threw /θru:/	thrown /θrəʊn/
understand /ˌʌndəˈstænd/	understood /ˌʌndəˈstʊd/	understood /ˌʌndəˈstʊd/
wake up /ˈweɪk ˈʌp/	woke up /ˈwəʊk ˈʌp/	woken up /ˈwəʊkn ˈʌp/
wear /weə(r)/	wore /wɔ:(r)/	worn /wɔ:n/
win /wɪn/	won /wʌn/	won /wʌn/
write /raɪt/	wrote /rəʊt/	written /ˈrɪtn/